CO

MODEL
BOATS

R. H. Warring

RADIO CONTROLLED MODEL BOATS

MODEL & ALLIED PUBLICATIONS
ARGUS BOOKS LIMITED

Model and Allied Publications
Argus Books Ltd.,
14 St. James Road,
Watford, Herts.

First Published 1981.

© R. H. Warring, 1981.
© Argus Books Ltd.

ISBN 0 85242 569 4

Printed by McCorquodale (Newton) Ltd., Newton-le-Willows, Lancashire.

CONTENTS

CHAPTER 1

RADIO CONTROL SYSTEMS FOR BOATS

A radio control system consists of a *Transmitter* and *Receiver* pre-tuned to respond to signals generated by the transmitter, and one or mcre *Servos* which convert the radio signals decoded by the receiver into mechanical output movements for the operation of various controls. All modern radio control systems are of *proportional* type, meaning that any particular movement of a transmitter control is converted into a corresponding or *proportional* output movement of the servo. In other words, this is like 'full size' controls—a certain movement of a steering wheel, say, providing a corresponding movement of a rudder. But it is *remote* control, with only the receiver and servo part of the radio system installed in the model, together with its associated batterv.

The number of controls a particular Transmitter/Receiver combination (known as a 'Combo') can operate is dependent on the number of *channels* it provides. The simplest is a 1-channel system—i.e. capable of working just *one* servo (e.g. for rudder control). Most manufacturers start with a 2-channel system in their range. A 2-channel Combo is capable of working *two* servos and offering *two* controls which can be operated quite independently and if necessary simultaneously—e.g. for rudder and 'engine' control with powerboats.

Single-stick 2-channel Transmitters are in the minority. Most 2-channel transmitters are two stick. A single-stick 2-channel transmitter is quite suitable for powerboat controls, using the side to side movement of the stick for rudder control and the up-and-down movement of the stick for throttle control (or electric motor switching). A single-stick 2-channel transmitter is not suitable for yachts, however. There is always the chance of accidentally—and unwantedly—altering the sail setting when using side-to-side movement for operating rudder control. So always choose a twin-stick (or wheel) transmitter for yachts.

More elaborate systems then progressively offer 3-channel, 4-channel, 5-channel, 6-channel, 7-channel and 8-channel coverage. Cost increases with the number of channels provided by a Combo—and a separate servo is needed to 'work' each channel, again adding to total cost. For boats a 3-channel Combo is usually more than adequate (see Chapter 2).

Here several important points arise in choosing your first radio control outfit. The cost of Combos is not directly proportional to the number of channels they provide. Thus a 3-channel Combo may not be very much more expensive than a 2-channel Combo; and a 4-channel Combo not much more than a 3-channel Combo. Try to think ahead as to the number of control functions you are likely to need for present *and* future models. If you think that a 2-channel Combo will be adequate, then settle for that. But if you think that you will probably go to three controls for your next model, then a 3-channel Combo will be a better initial buy, even if you only need 2 channels at the time. You can buy this with just two servos for your initial requirements—and buy another servo later when you want to advance to a 3-channel system.

The second point is that having bought a Combo, you do not need to buy a second Combo for a second model, and so on, assuming you want to leave the original receiver and servo installation intact in the first model. All you need for the second model is a second receiver and further servos to match. The same transmitter will do.

This, of course, applies only to the same *make* and/or model of Combo, second receiver and matching servos. It is unlikely that make 'X' transmitter will operate make 'Y' receiver and that make 'Z' servos will work with it. Rather like a camera system with its matching lenses, etc, you need to stick to the same make to expand your radio system around an initial Combo.

The third point is that with 2- and 3-channel Combos particularly there is usually a choice of 'all-drycell' or 'all-Nicad' versions. All-drycell Combos are considerably cheaper initially because they avoid the relatively high cost of Nicad batteries for the Transmitter and Receiver. They work off dry batteries.

In the long run an all-Nicad outfit will prove cheaper, since dry batteries need frequent replacement. Nicads do not, since they are rechargeable. After working through about a dozen sets of dry batteries, you will have spent more on buying and operating your radio than the original cost of an all-Nicad outfit.

It is possible, of course, to operate *two* boats simultaneously from a *single* twin-stick transmitter. Thus a 4-channel transmitter could provide two controls operated by one stick in one boat; and two controls operated by the other stick in another boat. Each boat would, of course, need to have its separate receiver and servos. Similarly a 5-channel Tx could provide two controls in one boat and three in another; and a 6-channel Tx three controls each in two separate boats.

Working more than one boat from a single transmitter has its limitations. An experienced *single* operator can cope quite well with two boats, provided they are both slow-moving displacement types. *Two* operators sharing the *same* transmitter are likely to find such a system awkward to work.

Two-channel radio provides full functional control for most boats. Preferred type of transmitter is twin-stick, each stick movement operating one control (top). Steerwheel transmitter (bottom) is not so popular with boat modellers.

Transmitter, Receiver and Servos all incorporate sophisticated electronic circuitry; and Servos also quite complicated mechanical devices. All such items are thus purchased ready made—i.e. as a standard proprietary Combo plus matching Servos, or complete outfits as they are called. The scope for home-constructed radio control equipment is strictly limited, although some outfits are available in kit

1.1

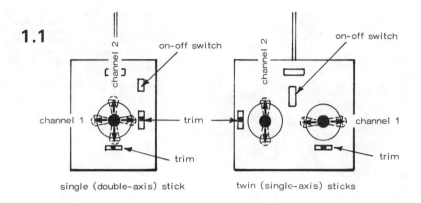

single (double-axis) stick   twin (single-axis) sticks

form. These can provide a saving in initial cost, but can present problems in checking and servicing if they do not work properly when built. For most modellers the best advice is invariably to purchase ready-made proprietary outfits.

Battery Power

Many radio control manufacturers offer a choice of 'all drycell' or 'Nicad' with 2- and 3-channel coverage. 'All-drycell' outfits work off standard dry batteries (usually type AA). However battery life is short, so frequent replacements are called for; also an all-drycell combo is not really suitable for operating more than two servos in a boat installation. The serious radio modeller is better advised to start with an 'all Nicad' outfit which has re-chargeable nickel-cadmium batteries. Not only will these batteries normally last for years, recharging when required, but their capacity is greater than drycells and the reliability of the whole system much better.

In both cases a single battery pack powers the Transmitter and a second battery pack powers both receiver and servos. Some special-duty servos (e.g. sail winches) may require a separate battery for working.

Transmitter Controls

Having been developed initially for model aircraft control the standard pattern adopted for transmitter controls is a pivoted stick, movable in one plane (i.e. up or down, *or* left and right) for a 1-channel system. For a 2-channel system the stick is pivoted in two axes or 'universally' (i.e. any amount of up or down movement controlling one channel can be associated with any amount of left or right movement controlling the other channel). Alternatively a 2-channel transmitter may have two sticks, each controlling its own channel. These alternatives are shown in Fig. 1.1.

10

1.2

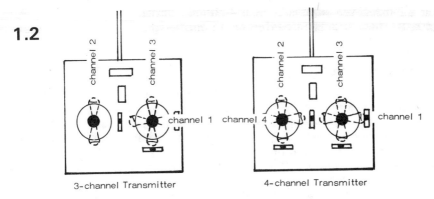

3-channel Transmitter   4-channel Transmitter

note: channel allocation may vary with different
makes of transmitters

For a 3-channel transmitter, one stick would have a 'universal' movement (controlling 2 channels) and the second stick would be of single plane movement. A 4-channel transmitter would have two 'universally' pivoted sticks—Fig. 1.2.

Sticks can be spring centering, so that on release they return to their central or neutral position (and thus the corresponding control on the model also returns to neutral). Alternatively they can be fitted with a ratchet or friction braking device so that the stick remains in any position to which it is set, until readjusted manually. This is normally fitted on one stick movement only. A self-centering stick would be used for operating a rudder control (and also elevators and ailerons on aircraft). A ratchet-braked stick would normally be used as a throttle or engine speed control.

Transmitters offering such alternatives (usually 3-channel and upwards) may be referred to as 'throttle left' (mode 1) or 'throttle right' (mode 2), depending on the physical position of the throttle stick—Fig. 1.3. This is of more significance to aircraft controls than boats, although

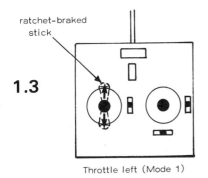

1.3

Throttle left (Mode 1)   Throttle right (Mode 2)

11

logically on a 2-stick system (whether 2-, 3- or 4-channel), 'throttle left' would be the choice for a right handed person and 'throttle-right' for a 'leftie' who prefers to steer with his left hand.

Trim Controls

Other controls associated with the stick controls are separate 'trims' in the form of small levers (for thumb operation) alongside each stick position. These provide for fine control movements for 'trimming', or effectively altering the 'neutral' position. In other words, if a model is 'pulling right', for example, instead of having to hold in a certain amount of left rudder all the time on the rudder stick, the rudder trim is moved to the left to set the required amount of correction with the rudder stick remaining in the neutral position.

Steerwheel Transmitters

Some manufacturers produce transmitters with a wheel steering control instead of a stick, particularly with model boats (and cars) in mind. This would appear an obvious favourite for boats—e.g. wheel steering of powerboats. Strangely, however, such systems have not found much favour with boat modellers, the majority of whom prefer stick controls. In fact the availability of 'steerwheel' type transmitter controls is very restricted.

The 'electronics' involved are exactly the same. Control stick movement moves a potentiometer a proportional amount. In the case

Three-channel radio is desirable when you want to incorporate additional working features on a model. All transmitters in this category are twin-stick.

of a stick, the stick movement acts at right angles to the potentiometer spindle. With a wheel movement, the wheel is mounted directly onto the potentiometer spindle. Thus it is well within the capabilities of an ingenious modeller with mechanical skills to convert a stick-controlled movement into a wheel-controlled movement if he so desires. This is easiest done where the original (stick) movement is a one-plane (1-channel) movement.

Receivers

The receiver is pretrimmed and needs no adjustment whatsoever. It is 'matched' to the transmitter 'sending' frequency by a crystal, which is normally removable and replaceable with crystals of other 'spot' frequencies. At the same time the transmitter crystal would have to be charged to match. This is to give the opportunity of simultaneous operation of several different radio controlled models with the same (permitted) frequency band-normally 27 MHz in Britain. Conventional AM sets then provide up to 12 'spot' frequencies, and FM sets up to 30 different 'spot', frequencies.

It is important to remember when changing crystals that they must always be changed in matched pairs, and that the transmitter crystal is of a slightly *different* frequency than the receiver crystal. In other words, given a crystal pair, only the *transmitter* crystal should be fitted to the transmitter, and the *receiver* crystal to the receiver.

Servos

Servos are normally designed to respond to the output of particular receivers. Thus transmitter and receiver manufacturers also produce matching servos. Avoid trying to use servos of different make to the transmitter/receiver Combo, unless they are specifically stated to be usable.

The servo is basically an electric motor driving an output arm or disc through reduction gearing, and controlled by sophisticated electronic circuits in the receiver and/or servo itself. Again it is an item which needs no adjustment or attention during normal use. If it develops a fault this can only be dealt with by returning to a service agent.

Servo output movements are of two types—*linear* where a lever arm or pair of arms traverses backwards and forwards in a push-pull movement; or *rotary* where the wheel is in the form of a disc or T-shaped arm, rotating for up to 45 degrees clockwise and anti-clockwise (90 degrees in all) about a neutral position. Both have their particular applications, but *rotary* output servos are the more common type.

A servo movement is usually self-centering. That is, it is controlled by a spring-centred stick on the transmitter. Movement of the stick one way makes the servo run one way; movement of the stick the other way makes the servo run the other way. The stick has to be moved to and held in a particular position to hold on the required amount of servo movement. If the stick is released it will return to its central position automatically, and the servo will follow it by returning to its neutral position.

If the stick has a 'braked' movement, then it will stop in any position to which it is moved, with the servo following accordingly. There is no *positive* selection of 'neutral' position as such. Merely provision to *adjust* the servo output to stop at any position from full movement one way to full movement the other way. The stick does not then have to be touched again until further adjustment is called for.

This is the standard form of a *throttle* control. It *can* also be used for rudder control on displacement type boats and yachts, with the advantage that once a certain amount of helm has been put on for holding a course the stick can be left until further steering control is required. This is rather like handling a full size boat (where the rudder is not self-centering). But it is not taking full advantage of the control channel available. In the absence of a helmsman actually aboard the model, it is *very* useful to have a self-centering rudder. And any rudder *trim* movement necessary can be set up by adjustment of the *trim control* associated with that particular stick on the transmitter. For these reasons all model boat rudders should (normally) be operated by a self-centering servo (i.e. controlled by a self-centering stick or wheel on the transmitter).

Retract Servos

A *retract servo* behaves differently to a standard servo. It is really designed to work from a single *non-proportional* channel signal. When signalled 'on' it will run from one extreme of movement to the other and stop there. When signalled 'off' it will run back to its original position and stop there. It will not stop in any intermediate position.

The usual method of signalling this channel is a toggle or rocker switch on the transmitter. It can also be controlled by a proportional channel stick. In this case, as soon as the stick is moved one way, the retract servo is signalled 'on', run to its extreme position and stay there, as long as the stick continues to be held that way. On release of the stick it will drive to its opposite extreme position. It cannot be stopped in any intermediate position. Also it will only respond to stick movement in *one* direction, not the other.

Retract servos have been developed specifically for aircraft, i.e. for operating retractable undercarriages. They have limited application in boats, except to utilise a *non-proportional channel* which may be available on the transmitter for operating an auxiliary service where the higher power and (usually) greater output movement (180 degrees

14

A number of 2- and 3-channel radio 'Combos' are available for either drycell or Nicad battery operation. Drycell versions are considerably cheaper to buy, but Nicad sets are preferred for all types of boats.

Protective cases are available for some transmitters. They are useful for protection against rain or spray.

instead of 90 degrees on a rotary servo) of a retract servo can be an advantage. However, an *ordinary* servo will work in just the same way as a retract servo if plugged into this non-proportional channel.

Special Servos and Controllers

Special servos have been developed for radio controlled boat applications. These are of two main types—sail winches for sheet hauling; and speed controllers for electric (propulsion) motors. Both are relatively expensive items but provide sophisticated additional controls, the performance of which cannot be matched by simpler systems.

Sail winches are basically similar to conventional servos, but with continuous rotary output movement clockwise or anti-clockwise with one or two drums on the output spindle. The use of two drums of different diameter gives different hauling speeds and travels for jib and main sheet adjustment from a single winch. They are generally larger, heavier and considerably more powerful than conventional control servos and may require a separate battery for operation to avoid 'overloading' the receiver battery.

Modern *Speed Controllers* designed to provide proportional speed control of electric (propulsion) motors from full ahead through stop to full astern are based on sophisticated digital electronic circuitry which feeds pulses of current to the motor at high frequency. The speed at which the motor runs is then determined by the 'mark-space' ratio of the pulses, which in turn is set by the transmitter control. Full throttle position on the transmitter would produce a 100:0 mark-space ratio signal from the speed controller, equivalent to a continuous current being fed to the motor. Backed off from the full throttle position the mark-space ratio signal from the speed controller would then progressively introduce more 'space' or 'motor off' time in the current output to the motor resulting in a progressively slower motor speed. As the pulses are generated at a very rapid rate there would be no apparent hesitation in the running of the motor. Finally on reaching 0:100 mark-space ratio, the output would be 'all off', and the motor would stop. By a further extension of the same principle of working the controller can also be made capable of providing speed control in the reverse running direction for 'astern' working. Here it is desirable to limit the maximum speed available (i.e. to less than a 100:0 mark-space ratio signal).

The speed controller is controlled directly by the receiver responding to the transmitter signal, as far as establishing the mark-space ratio is concerned. The output circuit of the controller, however, has to carry the current from a separate battery supplying the propulsion motor, so must have a suitable high rating. It is also usually necessary for the speed controller to incorporate a heat sink to dissipate the consider-

16

able heating produced by the circuits carrying heavy currents.

There are simpler types of speed controllers, e.g. based on potentiometers, but few are available as ready-made items. Possibilities in this direction are described in Chapter 7.

Wiring Connections

All modern radio control outfits are 'pre-wired' in the sense that a single wiring harness (supplied with a Combo) connects receiver and receiver battery by suitable plug-together connections. An on-off switch is also pre-connected in the wiring harness. Servos are supplied with their leads terminating in a plug to fit into appropriate sockets in the receiver. No additional wiring up at all is thus normally necessary to complete the radio installation. Servos and battery simply plug into the receiver.

Control Linkages

Servo output movements are connected to the rudder, throttle, or other services they are required to operate by mechanical links. These normally take the form of *push rods,* (rigid rods in metal, or wood with wire end fittings); or flexible cables in plastic tubes, known as *snakes.* Either type is considerably superior to cables of cord or thin flexible wire.

This particular aspect of radio control installation is described in detail in Chapter 3.

Traditional ply and hardwood construction is still favoured by many powerboat modellers. Kits reduce building time substantially by providing precut frames, bulkheads and other parts.

CHAPTER 2

BOAT TYPES AND CONTROLS

Working model boats fall into two main categories—*power boats* and *yachts.* Powerboats further subdivide into two main classes—*displacement* craft and *planing* craft. All types make excellent subjects for radio control, but actual control requirements do differ. The one common requirement is *rudder* as a primary (functional) control.

Displacement Boats

Displacement type power boats range in size from about 15 inches long up to several feet in length. The only real limit to length is set by the weight and transportability of large models. Types may range from simple runabouts or cabin cruisers to scale warships, etc—all normally powered by electric motors.

Since their operating speeds are quite moderate just rudder control may be adequate (especially for small craft), requiring only a 1-channel (1-function outfit) and a single servo on the radio side (in practice a 2-

Even quite small powerboats — under 22" in length — can accommodate 2-channel radio quite successfully.

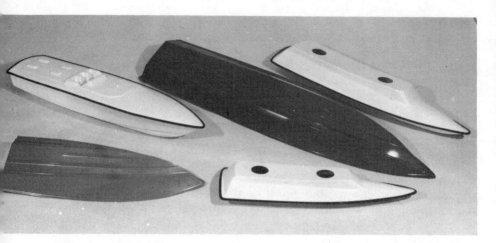

Modellers in a hurry to complete their boats can buy moulded hulls with matching decks, ready to fit out with power unit and radio. These are examples of racing hulls moulded in glassfibre.

channel outfit with just one servo). A 2-channel system is much to be preferred, however, on all hulls large enough to take a second servo to provide at least on-off switching of the main propulsion motor(s); and preferably forward-stop-reverse switching. An electric motor *speed controller* is even better for the second (motor) control function as this is capable of providing variable speeds forward and astern. The only drawback in this case is the cost of such a special type of servo, which can be as high as that of the Transmitter-Receiver Combo itself.

Larger displacement craft, and particularly scale models, can also be made more interesting by providing additional secondary controls. Ideally these should be quite separate from the main functional controls—i.e. rudder and propulsion motor control—and thus operated via an additional radio channel or channels. The obvious solution of using a Combo with more channels, and an additional servo for operating *each* secondary control, is not necessarily the best in such cases as cost can mount appreciably. There are simpler and less costly solutions which can be adopted and the subject of secondary controls is covered in more detail in Chapter 8.

Planing Craft

Planing type power boats are normally powered by i/c engines (diesel or glow). Again sizes may range from about 15 inches upwards, although maximum length in this case is unlikely to exceed about 48 inches because of the size of engines available. The usual maximum engine size is .60 cu. in. (10cc), although larger engines are available and may be used in larger craft.

20

Rudder control is obviously essential, and because of the high operating speeds of such models, engine control is almost equally essential. This means that the engine used should be of throttled type (referred to as a R/C engine or an engine with a throttle-type carburettor). This throttle control can be operated by a second servo to give a range of operating speeds forward, plus 'stop engine' as well if desired (see Chapter 6 on i/c engine controls). Thus a minimum R/C outfit for this type of model is a 2-channel Combo plus two servos.

Additional controls may or may not be desirable. In the cases of *racing* powerboats adjustable transom tabs (trim tabs) can be extremely helpful in achieving maximum performance, especially under difficult sea conditions. Normally adjusted tabs can be used to trim a model for particular conditions, but making the tabs adjustable whilst running via radio control provides full control of trim all the time. Because transom tabs used in this way are a primary functional control they should be operated via a separate channel—in this case calling for a 3-channel Combo and 3 servos, or a 4-channel Combo and 4 servos if the full potential of transom tabs is to be used (see later).

Not all i/c engined craft are designed for 'racing' performance, however. An i/c engine may be used in a large scale model to give near scale speed performance, for example an electric motor not having enough power to do this economically. This would again call for a minimum of a 2-channel outfit. Then further secondary controls may be added, such as operation of lights, gun traversing, etc. See Chap. 8.

Fast Electrics

The advent of high-power electric motors and high-energy Nicad (nickel-cadmium) rechargeable cells has made possible the development of electric-powered boats capable of full planing performance — a type known as 'fast electrics'. Speeds achieved, in fact, can be comparable with that of i/c engined powerboats, but in somewhat smaller, lighter hulls. They also have their own competition classes for speed, steering and 'multi' racing.

For competition work, at least, radio control is essential with a fast electric boat, calling for 2-channel equipment covering rudder and motor control. Both are essential for covering courses as speed. 'Stepped' motor speed controls may be used, but full proportional speed control of the electric motor is recommended.

Yachts

Rudder control can transform the performance of even simple model yachts, compared with free sailing, and even compensate for minor faults in sail setting. It gives the model yachtsman the ability to tack, avert collisions with other craft using the same water, and keep away from unfavourable areas where sailing conditions are poor. It also means that the yacht can be headed smartly into the wind to avoid a blowdown when hit by a heavy gust.

The courses that can be sailed, however, are still very much restricted by the initial sail setting. The simplest course is a reach which may be repeatable from side to side across the pond—but usually only with some gain or loss of 'way' or position relative to the launching spot. Another setting will give the possibility of a complete course to windward, tacking from side to side—but this means that the model will have to be retrieved and re-trimmed at the end of the beat. Similarly with a run before the wind. Again rudder will be most useful in keeping the yacht on course—but a re-start with new sail settings is necessary at the end of the run.

Obviously *complete* functional control of a model yacht thus needs rudder plus sail trimming—i.e. a 2-channel outfit. The second servo is then used to adjust sails through suitable mechanisms working as sheet hauls, or can be in the form of a *sail winch* with direct hauling capabilities—see Chapters 9 and 10.

The racing model yachtsman may well find it an advantage—or even necessary—to adopt 3-channel radio. The third servo can then be used for controlling the jib sheet independently of the main sheet for optimum sail trimming. In practice the second servo would normally be used to adjust both jib and main sheets simultaneously via a sail winch. The third servo would then be used for further adjustment of the jib sheet, as necessary (see Chapter 9).

Experimental and Unorthodox

Some individual types of model boats do not fall into any of the categories previously described, and may set special requirements, or

Fast electrics — high speed powerboats fitted with electric motors — are a growing interest. They can be used with 1- and 2-channel radio.

Scale offshore powerboat model, capable of high speeds with i-c engine power, needs radio control for safe operation.

special problems for outfitting with radio control. Again these can be examined in the light of what controls are necessary *functionally* (i.e. to maintain proper control of the craft) and those which merely add interest features (secondary services or controls).

Submarines represent a particular case in point. These really need four primary controls, viz:

(i) Rudder for steering

(ii) Motor speed control—forward and stop; but preferably also including reverse.

(iii) Hydrovane inclination, or 'diving' trim control.

(iv) Water ballast emptying, for diving and surfacing.

In practice it is possible to reduce these to three functions using a fixed amount of ballast (equivalent appreciably to 'deck awash' trim) and relying on forward speed and hydroplane inclination to control dive.

The more ambitious modeller might then be tempted to add at least one secondary function—e.g. torpedo launching.

Special problems which then arise are:—

(i) Maintenance of control when submerged. Theoretically radio contact will be lost as soon as the aerial is submerged (or 'earthed' by immersion in water if a bare wire aerial is used). In practice this loss of control is not necessarily complete. Nevertheless some built-in safety feature is necessary in order to ensure that should control be lost the model submarine will not continue diving forwards and downwards, but will rise to the surface.

In practice, control of a submarine can usually be maintained to depths of about 6-9 feet, within 30 feet of the operator,

provided the aerial wire is *completely* insulated from the surrounding water.

(ii)   *Complete* watertightness of all radio compartments, so that water cannot get in via control linkage outlets for example.

(iii)   'Fail safe' feature(s) in the event of battery failure. If this cannot be arranged to ensure rising to the surface (e.g. failure of the system automatically blows the ballast tanks), then a simple wreck buoy release can be used. This can be a purely 'mechanical' release independent of motor control. Then, if the hull remains watertight, the model can be recovered unharmed via the wreck buoy.

Airscrew Driven Boats

Airscrew driven boats are invariably light, high speed planing craft, so rudder control is highly desirable. However, since many of this type are quite small, powered by .049 or in similar motor sizes, the hull may not be large enough to accommodate the weight of radio gear without destroying the performance.

24

This is no longer a problem in larger hulls, when engine speed (throttle) control can also be added to advantage, but again weight must be kept to a minimum in order to achieve maximum performance. In general, size for size and motor for motor, a radio controlled airscrew driven hydroplane will not be as fast as its free running counterpart because of the weight penalty of the additional radio gear. It is far safer to operate this type of model under radio control rather than free

running, however, especially on water used by other craft. So this type has an appeal both as a 'fun' and 'racing' model.

However, airscrew driven boats are not accepted by the Model Power Boat Association, and are also looked upon with disfavour by most local authorities.

Catamarans

The sailing *catamaran* is also picked out as a special type because its handling characteristics differ from those of conventional yachts, especially if it is a 'racing' type (i.e. lightly constructed with generous sail area).

The main thing about sailing a catamaran is that a capsize can be disastrous—and can happen all too easily in strong winds especially as the best trim for maximum speed is sailing with one hull raised completely free from the water. Once capsized a catamaran will stay upside down and unless the radio compartment is completely watertight, water seepage into the transmitter, servo(s) and battery is almost inevitable if recovery is delayed for any appreciable time. The large hollow float carried on the top of the sail of some full size catamarans to prevent complete capsize is not really a practical proposition on a model. It needs to be excessively large to be effective.

The other type of capsize common with fast model catamarans is when one hull dips bow under suddenly, literally somersaulting the craft into a capsize. This is largely a matter of trim (assuming the hull design is satisfactory). Adding ballast to the aft end of each hull to bring the centre of gravity farther back is a preventive measure, but no complete answer.

It is also necessary to get the centre of gravity or balance point of a catamaran at a point equivalent between the hulls. A sideways offset centre of gravity will aggravate any tendency to capsize in one direction (i.e. towards the nearest hull).

Whilst capsize is not directly concerned with radio control it has been described at some length since radio can provide the helmsman

Example of an advanced radio controlled model boat system available in kit form. The smaller daughter ship can be launched and recovered by the larger rescue ship, and both can be operated independently under radio control.

26

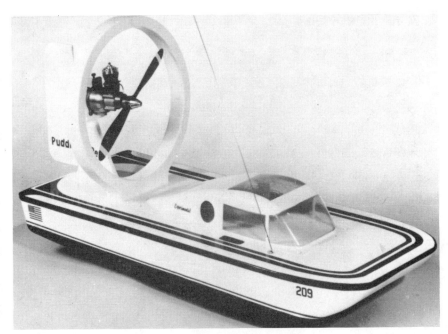

Unusual amphibian, available as a kit model, and designed for radio control.

Hovercraft might also be a subject for radio control but the payload they can carry successfully is limited.

Yachts are another type of model which literally ask to be radio controlled. Far better — and more reliable — than vane steering for racing.

with means of dealing with an imminent capsize. Rudder control alone is not fully effective in this respect. It will enable the helmsman to attempt a smart turn into wind to release pressure on the sails and lose speed, but the drag of the lower hull when a model catamaran is starting a capsize may overcome the turning effect of the rudder, so that the craft still drives on and over.

Conventional sheet winching will also not be fast enough for emergency action—so a special additional feature which can be well worth considering is a rapid mainsheet release to deal with such happenings. It needs to be reversible so that the sheet can be hauled in again to reset to normal sailing trim.

Model size, again, is important. The smaller the model catamaran, the less effective radio control is likely to be. This, in fact, applies to almost all types of model boats. Radio control incorporated in a small model can be more of a novelty feature than a really rewarding exercise. The safety of the model—and its expensive radio gear—is also more in danger through smaller freeboard and the relatively larger size of even small wavelets.

It does not automatically follow that 'the bigger the model the better', but for serious radio control working, 30-36 inches hull length is about a minimum size to consider. Then, both from portability and propulsion motor performance in the case of power boats, a length of about 54 inches is a possible maximum size for easy handling.

Using Transom Flaps (Trim Tabs)

Transom flaps or trim tabs are only normally used on fast planing powerboats (but they can also prove effective on some displacement hulls, to correct heel). They are *trim* controls, and can be in two ways. Moving (or adjusting) both flaps in the same way provides control of fore-and-aft trim. Lowering the flaps pushes the bow down. Raising both flaps lifts the bow up. Lowering one flap only (or lowering

Some scale R-C boats are fast-moving. This one is powered by triple electric motors.

29

Submarines are not excluded as subjects for radio control. Main problem here is in achieving complete watertightness of the hull and radio compartment.

one and raising the other) works in a similar manner to ailerons on an aircraft. It makes the hull roll or 'bank' in one direction then the other. Thus to take full advantage of transom flaps you need to be able to operate them simultaneously (both moving together in the same direction); or differentially (aileron type movement).

The use of transom flaps for fore-and-aft trim on model powerboats is different to that on full size powerboats. Their main use on a model is to eliminate 'porpoising' or the development of violent pitching motion when a model is running in choppy water. This normally means trimming out with an optimum amount of *down* flap, which gives maximum running speed. On a full size powerboat, down flap is mostly used to provide additional lift at the stern to enable the craft to come onto plane as soon as possible. It can also be useful to help keep the bow down and reduce porpoising when heading into a sea at high speed, but as far as (full size) *racing* performance is concerned, transom flaps are trimmed as far *up* as possible to give minimum hull resistance through the water.

A model powerboat with hull lines similar to a full size powerboat and operating on *dead calm* water should show similar characteristics. Inching the flaps up carefully, a little at a time, should give an increase in speed – up to the point where 'up' trim is excessive and the craft tends to become directionally unstable.

Using the flaps for 'banking' trim is fairly obvious. Lowering one flap will produce more lift at the stern on that side, rolling the hull in the opposite direction. At the same time, the extra drag will tend to induce a turn to that side, which may need a little *rudder* trim movement to compensate on a shallow-vee hull. In fact, excessive differential movements on transom flaps will tend to produce a turn with the hull rolling into an *opposite* bank. However, a deep-vee hull will correct this by reacting to the ensuing sideslip.

There will also be some lower speed at which flap action may become reversed. The 'down' flap will then generate more 'drag' than 'lift' and pull the model round into the opposite direction expected.

The reaction of flaps on high speed hulls is thus not always as simple as may appear at first sight, particularly if they have differential as well as simultaneous movement. It is best to start with a reasonably large size of flap (say one quarter of the transom width for each flap) and *small* movements. Flap area can then be trimmed down, as found necessary, or desirable. If this makes them a little too ineffective, then the movement can be increased.

CHAPTER 3

SERVOS AND LINKAGES

Modern proportional servos are all generally similar in appearance and performance, although sizes may range from very small 'micro' servos with a case size of about $1\frac{1}{4}$ in x 1 in x $\frac{1}{2}$ in to 'mammoth' (case size about 3 in x $1\frac{1}{2}$ in). The more general case size is about $1\frac{3}{4}$ in x $1\frac{1}{2}$ in x $\frac{3}{4}$ in. As a rough guide the size of servo case is a rough indication of the size of the motor it contains, and thus the *output effort* it can produce, although this is also dependent on the output gear ratio incorporated. Standard type (aircraft) servos are generally powerful enough to operate all the controls required on model boats, except for sail winching duties on large yachts and rudders on really large powered craft.

Servos are classified as *rotary* or *linear,* depending on their output movements. A *rotary* servo has a disc mounted on the output spindle, drilled with lines of holes offering alternative positions for linking up a pushrod. It is usually supplied with an alternative T-shaped arm or arms—Fig. 3.1.

Maximum output movement is usually of the order of 45 degrees either side of its neutral position Transit time, or time to travel from neutral to full movement position, may range from 0.25 seconds to 0.5 seconds, depending on the particular type and purpose for which it is primarily designed. Servos for operating high loads may have slower operating speeds to achieve a greater force output through higher reduction gearing.

The *resolution* and *self-centering* characteristics of a servo are also important. *Resolution* is the ability to follow movement of the Tx control stick faithfully. Nearly all modern proportional servos have high

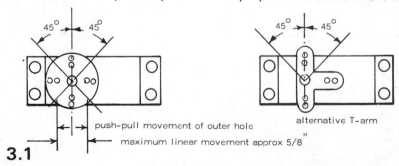

push-pull movement of outer hole

maximum linear movement approx 5/8"

alternative T-arm

3.1

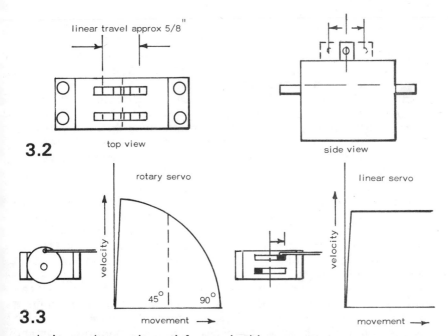

3.2 top view side view

linear travel approx 5/8"

rotary servo linear servo

velocity velocity

45° 90°

3.3 movement → movement →

resolution and are quite satisfactory in this respect.

Self-centering refers to the response of a servo when it automatically returns to its neutral position (e.g. when a self-centering Tx stick is released). Ideally it should stop dead at the neutral position (i.e. not 'hunt' one way and the other about neutral before it stops). Also it should stop exactly at the *same* neutral position each time. Most servos are satisfactory in the first respect. Some are not so good as others in providing an exact neutral. A servo which is bad in this respect should not be used for rudder control on high speed craft.

A *linear* servo is similar in general appearance, except for the output movement. This is a lug (or more usually two lugs) traversing slots in the top of the case. Typical movement is about $\frac{5}{16}$ in. either side of the centre (neutral) position (or $\frac{5}{8}$ in. total travel)—Fig. 3.2.

Both a rotary and a linear servo can equally well perform the same duty, e.g. operate a rudder or a throttle equally well. In many cases it is just a matter of which type is more convenient to install. There is a subtle difference in the actual output movements, however. The actual point from which the output movement is produced in a rotary servo moves through an arc and so the resulting *velocity* of the push rod is not constant even if the disc (or arm) rotates at a constant speed. The push-pull output from a linear servo, however, produces a constant velocity movement of the push rod—Fig. 3.3. It is thus more precise in terms of *true* proportional control movement although the difference is hardly noticed in practice.

Both types of servos respond in the same way. Movement of the transmitter control stick in one direction causes the servo output to rotate one way (or the arm of a linear servo to traverse in one direction). Movement of the transmitter stick in the other direction reverses the direction of movement of the servo.

Servos are invariably pre-wired to plugs ready to plug into a matching receiver. Their direction of response to transmitter stick movement is therefore pre-determined by the way they are wired up initially. Identical servos are usually available with opposite-hand wiring to respond the opposite way round. (Some transmitters, usually only the more expensive multi-channel type, may incorporate switching for reversing the response direction of servos).

The significance of this is that a servo as supplied, and plugged into a receiver will respond either with 'clockwise' or 'anticlockwise' movement. It is necessary to check which way round it works before connecting to a control as it may give opposite control response to that required. For example study Fig. 3.4 which shows a simple link-up of a servo to operate a rudder.

When the transmitter control stick is moved to the left, say, to call for left rudder, all is well if the servo responds by rotating in a *clockwise* direction (diagram A). If, on the other hand, the servo response is to rotate in an *anticlockwise* direction, then the command 'left rudder' will, in fact, produce *right* rudder (diagram B).

Fortunately there are simple alternative solutions should such reversal of control response occur. The obvious one is to replace the servo with its 'opposite hand' counterpart, if available. If not, it is merely a matter of changing the output point to the opposite side of the disc (Fig. 3.5A); or refitting the tiller arm on the opposite side (Fig. 3.5B). If a throttle control is concerned, an alternative solution is to

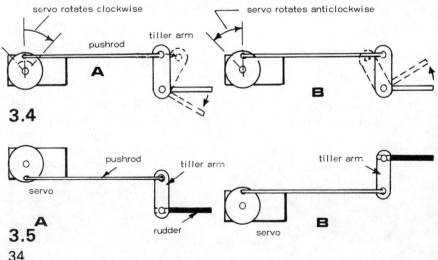

3.4

3.5

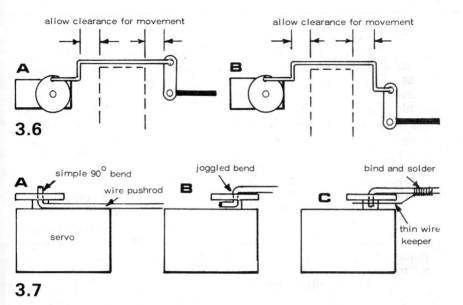

3.6

3.7

reposition the servo on the opposite side of the throttle arm to reverse the movement.

Wire Push Rods

A push rod which connects a servo output to a tiller, throttle arm or other control movement is simply that—a rigid wire rod of the required length, bent to a suitable shape. It can also be a metal or plastic tube, or a wood dowel, etc, with suitable end fastenings. For model boats wire push rods are usually the simplest and most convenient type to use.

The *size* of wire to use is 16 swg. The preformed holes on proprietary servo output discs or arms are usually of a tight matching fit to this size, i.e. there will be no free play or slop in the pushrod movement. In some cases the fit may be a little *too* tight, in which case the servo output hole(s) may need *slightly* enlarging—e.g. by using a $\frac{1}{16}$" drill as a reamer pushed backward and forward through the hole(s).

The run of a push rod does not necessarily have to be straight. It can be cranked or otherwise bent to provide clearance around obstacles and still give the same positive movement—e.g. see Fig. 3.6. The only real limitation for boat installations is that steel wire (piano wire) which makes the strongest, most rigid push rods, is prone to rusting. Brass wire is better in this respect, but is much weaker and more readily bent out of shape accidentally, especially on a cranked run.

One real advantage of a wire pushrod is that suitable end fastenings can be formed by the wire itself. Fig. 3.7 shows three simple methods

35

of bending one end of a wire push rod to connect to the output of a rotary servo. Method A is the simplest, calling for only a 90 degree bend and using the top of the servo case to retain the wire in position. However, it is the *least* recommended since rubbing contact between the wire and a metal case is highly undesirable. It could generate 'noise' interfering with the operation of the radio receiver.

The method shown in Fig. 3.7B is almost as simple, but calls for an accurate Z bend which is more difficult to make. Once correctly made and fitted, it is virtually foolproof. Method Fig. 3.6 is probably the best general purpose solution. Again it only calls for a simple right angle bend. The push rod now lies on top of the output disc and must be retained in position with a separate 'keeper' of thin wire bound and soldered to the push rod. Alternatively, a proprietary keeper can be fitted to a wire push rod.

Similar methods of fitting can be used to attach the other end of the push rod to a tiller, but unless the second bend is made at *exactly* the right length, setting up the control properly can be almost impossible. The simple answer in such a case is to make the push rod to approximate length and then adjust the *servo* position as necessary to give central rudder position with the servo in the neutral position. In this case it is best to mount the servo sideways on hardwood bearers, so that its fore and aft positioning can readily be adjusted before finally screwing it to the bearers—Fig. 3.8A.

An alternative is to provide a Z bend in the arm of the pushrod which can be adjusted with pliers to shorten or lengthen the effective length of the push rod once installed—Fig. 3.8B.

Both methods are crude, however, and not generally to be recommended. It is better to have the second end fitting of a wire push rod adjustable. This means threading that end of the push rod to take a proprietary end fitting of the clevis (or similar) type. Adjustment of effective push rod length can then be made by screwing the end fitting in or out along the threaded position of the rod.

Clevis-type end fittings should be used with an output *arm* (or a control horn) rather than a disc—Fig. 3.9A—making sure that the

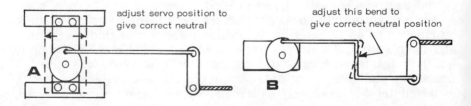

adjust servo position to give correct neutral

adjust this bend to give correct neutral position

A

B

3.8

36

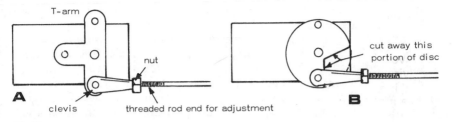

A — T-arm / nut / clevis / threaded rod end for adjustment

B — cut away this portion of disc

3.9

clevis cannot foul the top of the servo case over the full range of servo output movement. If a clevis is fitted to a *disc* output, then the disc usually needs to be cut away as shown in Fig. 3.9B. If not, unless the throat opening of the clevis is unusually long the rim of the disc will jam in the clevis with increasing rotation. This will tend to bend the clevis *sideways* rather than provide a continued push-pull movement and stall the movement completely. (If this is not clear, fit a clevis to a disc output and see how little pivotal movement actually is present before the clevis jams against the rim of the disc).

An important point to remember when adjusting a push rod to length is that the neutral position assumed by the servo may *be different when the radio is switched off* to when it is switched on. Thus make this final adjustment with *both* the receiver and transmitter switched on. Switching just the receiver on will probably make the servo move to a false 'neutral' position. Switching the transmitter on will then make it move to its true neutral position.

Proprietary Push Rods

Numerous proprietary push rods are available in metal and tubular plastic together with matching metal or plastic end fittings. These can produce neater, more professional looking installations, although they may mean certain limitations as regards mounting. Also the choice of suitable end fittings can be significant.

As a general rule pivoted joints in a control linkage should avoid metal-to-metal rubbing contact as otherwise these may produce interference signals or electrical 'noise'.

This is particularly likely to be noticed on powerboat installations where engine vibration will tend to generate vibratory rubbing contact at pivot points, especially where a throttle pushrod attaches to a throttle arm. Thus a *plastic* end fitting should be used on the end of a wire or metal pushrod connecting to a *metal* tiller or throttle arm. If a *metal* end fitting is used, it should connect to a *plastic* control arm or horn.

Proprietary clevises are normally self-locking so that they cannot spring apart and so accidentally become disconnected. If this self-locking action is not apparent, or appears too weak, then a binding of thin fuse wire, or even a small rubber band, can be added as a keeper.

It is essential with all pushrod movements that there should be no possibility of the movement being jammed in any way. This will stall the servo and draw excess current from the receiver battery. Equally important, all control movements should operate freely without binding, with friction reduced to the minimum possible. This will reduce the load on the servo(s) and consequently the drain on the receiver battery which powers the servo(s). The greater the load against which it has to work, the more current the servo will draw from the receiver battery. For example, a typical servo may draw about 15-25 milliamps when 'idling' and up to 100 milliamps when driving a control to position. If stalled during this process, current drain may rise to 250-350 milliamps.

Snakes

'Snake' is the name given to a flexible cable (Bowden cable) housed in an outer tube. The latter may be of metal or plastic. Plastic (PTFE) tubes are preferred as being free from corrosion and offering minimum resistance to movement of the inner cable.

A snake operates with a push-pull action, just like a push rod. The run of the cable can be curved, even turned back on itself, which can simplify control link up problems—Fig. 3.10. Action should also be as reliable as that of pushrods, provided the outer tube is rigidly mounted or supported at suitable intervals. The limitation of snakes is that at the extreme of a push movement the system is only as rigid as the rigidity of the flexible cable emerging from the end of the tube. For this reason a snake is less suitable for operating a rudder on larger or high speed craft where rudder loads may be high (although even here the use of a balanced rudder may make a snake perfectly feasible).

Proprietary snakes are available already assembled with end fittings.

operation of throttle control by a 'snake'

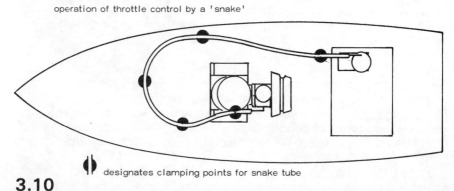

designates clamping points for snake tube

3.10

38

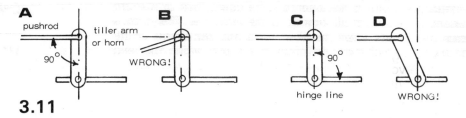

3.11

These are to be preferred to home-made types as soldering suitable end fittings to Bowden cable can prove tricky.

Alignment Requirements

Alignment of the pushrod ends, regardless of whether the rod is rigid or a snake, should be 'square' (i.e. at 90 degrees) to the servo output disc or arm, and the control horn or tiller arm, when the servo is in its neutral position—Fig. 3.11. This will ensure *equal* movements of the control either side of neutral, which is particularly important in the case of rudders. To ensure equal movements it is also important that

The range of servos matching Futaba 'M' series and 'L' series Tx/Rx Combos. These include water-resistant type for boats, a sail winch and a proportional speed controller for electric motors.

39

the attachment point of the pushrod to the control horn or tiller arm should be on a line at 90 degrees to the hinge line. This is not a problem with boats where the tiller arm is mounted directly on the rudder spindle which forms the hinge. It is a point which may need bearing in mind with other types of control surfaces operated by control horns or similar fittings.

CHAPTER 4

RADIO INSTALLATION

The two main requirements of any boat installation are (i) to locate the radio gear in such a position where it cannot get wet; and (ii) to locate the receiver as far as possible from sources of interference (e.g. electric motors). The latter is really only significant in the case of electric-powered boats. Servos, which themselves contain electric motors, can be located close to the receiver since they are fully suppressed. It is usually best, however, to plan installation of receiver, (radio) battery and servos as a compact 'pack' as this will make it easier to provide protection from water.

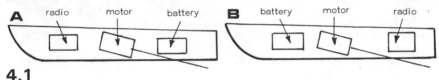

4.1

The dryest part of a hull should be the forward sections, e.g. under the foredeck—Fig. 4.1A. However this is not readily accessible and also calls for a long push rod to connect to the tiller. Usually the more practical choice is to locate the radio 'pack' well aft—Fig. 4.1B. This should provide conveniently short control runs and the whole radio section can be made accessible through a waterproof hatch. In the case of an electric-powered boat, the propulsion motor battery can be mounted forward, as necessary, to balance the weight of the radio gear. With an i/c engined boat, the fuel tank is usually mounted forward of the engine—Fig. 4.2. Note here that the control run to the engine throttle may have to be installed before decking in the hull—see chapter 6. Normally control runs require no servicing, except if accidentally bent or damaged, or an end link comes adrift. Thus

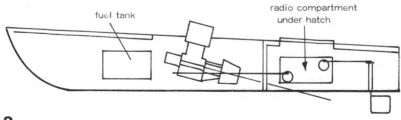

4.2

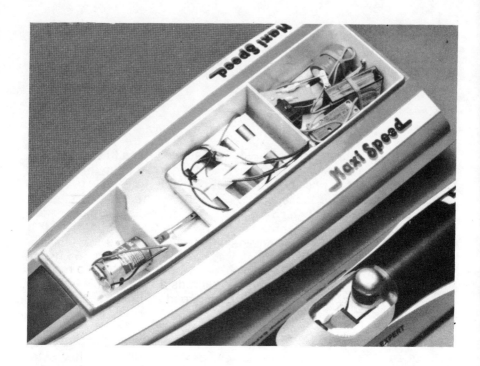

access is really only needed to the *ends* of control runs.

In the case of yachts the radio 'pack' is normally located amidships with a hatch of suitable size to give complete access to all the radio gear—see Chapter 9.

In quite a number of cases the radio components—receiver, servos and battery—are simply disposed at suitable positions throughout the hull. Servos adjacent to the controls they operate and the receiver and battery in any convenient position, for example. Only servos need positive fixing. They are mounted by screws passing through rubber grommets in the servo mounting lugs either onto hardwood bearers, or a ply tray with cut-outs (or a proprietary servo mount secured inside the hull). Receiver and battery should be wrapped in foam rubber and can then be laid in any suitable compartment.

This is the simplest method of installation, but certainly not the best. If it is adopted, then the *least* requirement is to mount the servos and support the receiver and battery well above the bilge area, i.e. in what should be a dry part of the hull. It is far better practice to locate all the radio components together in the form of a 'pack' in a watertight compartment.

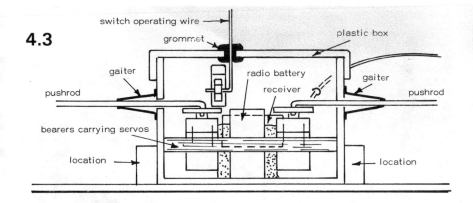

4.3

switch operating wire

grommet

plastic box

gaiter

radio battery

gaiter

pushrod

receiver

pushrod

bearers carrying servos

location

location

In all cases it should be possible to remove the complete radio gear after detaching the control rods at the servos. When a boat is not in use for some time and is stowed in a garage, say, it is best to remove the radio gear after detaching the control rods at the servos and store in a dry place indoors. That should be regarded as an essential part of laying-up procedure, especially during the winter months.

Undoubtedly the best way of mounting the radio gear is in a watertight box—Fig. 4.3. This can be a plastic sandwich box of suitable size; or special boxes are available as proprietary items for boat modellers. Only the servos need positive fixing inside the box. The receiver can be wrapped in foam (useful for protecting it against engine vibration); even the battery may be similarly treated and/or strapped in place with a rubber band. Just make sure that the receiver or battery cannot shift its position and foul a servo movement. Depending on the type of box used, servos may be fixed directly to the bottom of the box via double-sided servo tape; or to a wood tray or bearers glued inside the box. The box itself will also need some positive means of location in the hull to prevent it moving under back-pressure from servo operation.

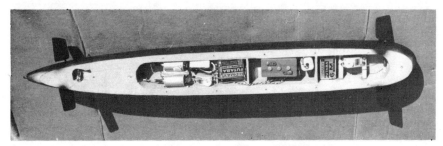

Complete installation of radio gear and drive motor in a radio controlled submarine.

43

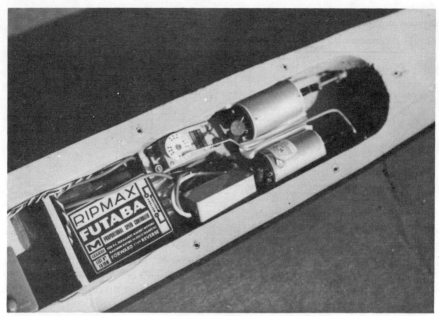

Model submarine controls include electronic speed controlled for drive motor.

Rudder servo and pushrod connecting to tiller arm.

An example of how NOT to fit out a small electric powered model. The 'brick' receiver incorporating an integral servo should have been mounted aft with a short push rod connecting to the rudder servo. Weight of this could then be balanced by mounting all batteries well forward.

Openings are required in the box for: (i) the servo pushrods to emerge; (ii) access to the on-off switch; and (iii) for the receiver aerial to emerge. A *slotted* hole is required to clear each pushrod to allow for sideways travel (e.g. to accommodate a rotary servo output movement; or a tiller arm movement, even if driven by a linear servo. Make sure that the slots are just large enough to clear the full *sideways* movement of the pushrods without binding. Only close-fitting holes are needed to pass 'snakes' through the box, though.

These openings can then be sealed by fitting rubber gaiters or miniature bellows—Fig. 4.4. Again these are available as proprietary items. They are designed to accommodate the full push-pull movement of the rod. This is better than using a rubber grommet which cannot provide a complete seal and will also add friction to the movement. Snake holes can be sealed with adhesive, although this will not adhere properly to a plastic snake tube.

The aerial wire presents no problem. It can be led through a hole carrying a tight-fitting rubber grommet and the grommet finish sealed with a *flexible* sealant of the type used for washbasin or bath surrounds. Do not seal with an adhesive which sets hard as this could eventually cause breakage of the strands in the aerial wire. For the

4.4

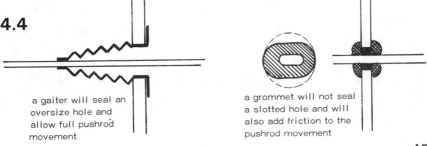

a gaiter will seal an oversize hole and allow full pushrod movement

a grommet will not seal a slotted hole and will also add friction to the pushrod movement

With the engine characteristically mounted well forward in an engine-powered fast boat, there is plenty of room for radio installation aft.

The easiest type of model to fit out with radio — a scale or semi-scale hard chine (electric powered) motor cruiser.

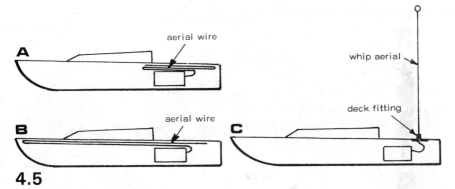

aerial wire

A

aerial wire

B

whip aerial

deck fitting

C

4.5

same reason, make sure that there is a certain amount of slack in the aerial wire between the lid of the box and the receiver.

Routing of the aerial wire from the point where it emerges from this box should avoid taking it near the drive motor in an electric-powered boat; and never *parallel* to any other electric wiring.

Accommodating the external run of aerial wire can be a problem in powerboats, since there is usually no mast or other convenient point to which the end can be run. The usual length of aerial wire is 30 inches. Cutting it shorter will reduce effective radio range; as also will coiling or doubling the wire up.

Quite satisfactory operation *may* be achieved with the aerial wire coiled up under the deck-Fig. 4.5A; or better still, doubled round the run of the deck inside the hull—Fig. 4.5B. This may prove troublesome on electric-powered boats, though, for it is desirable to keep the receiver aerial wire as far away as possible from an electric motor and the wiring carrying current to that motor. A more efficient solution is to cut the wire short and solder to a special metal deck fitting to take a 'whip' aerial—Fig. 4.5C. The whip in this case is a length of 18 or 20 gauge piano wire which is a tight plug fit in the deck fitting and can be removed for transport and storage. The top end of the whip should be fitted with a plastic button or tab, or better still bent into a closed loop, for safety reasons. Ideally the whole length of aerial (shortened aerial wire plus whip) should be the same as that of the original aerial wire. However, since a vertical wire whip is very efficient as an aerial, its length can be shortened if necessary.

The extension arm for the on-off switch can again be led through a tight fitting rubber grommet, or preferably a gaiter. Similar treatment is advised where the extension wire passes through the deck, but this is not essential.

Properly fitted out, a radio box of this type should be fully watertight—so much so, in fact, that it can actually provide buoyancy if the hull accidentally fills with water. It is not good practice to have the box permanently sealed, however. It is advisable to remove the lid

47

Moulded parts for making a watertight radio box produced by SHG. Kit also includes rubber bellows, sealing strip and fasteners.

The radio box fully assembled and mounted on a ply baseplate to demonstrate fitting.

Apart from saving building time, a great advantage of a moulded plastic hull is that the interior is uncluttered, even after fitting bulkheads and necessary stringers and installing motor(s) in their design position. That makes radio installation straightforward.

when the craft is not in use to let the radio compartment 'breathe'. A sealed box can produce heavy condensation inside with a drop in temperature. Inclusion of a sachet or two of silica gel (such as commonly supplied with cameras in their original boxes) will help ensure that the atmosphere in the box remains dry, even if left sealed for some considerable time.

Not all modellers may think that installation of the radio gear in a watertight box is worth the complication and adopt a simpler technique, such as enclosing the gear in a polythene bag. Pushrods and aerial wire then emerge from the open end of the bag, which is closed with a rubber band (the on-off switch can be operated through the bag). This method can have severe limitations. It is not fully waterproof and is very prone to develop condensation inside the bag. If employed, leave the neck of the bag open when the model is not in use.

Building a special watertight compartment integral with the hull to house the radio gear is another alternative, but this is really the same as the 'radio box' system and needs similar sealing treatment to be effective.

At the other end of the scale you can get away with straightforward mounting of the radio gear under the hull with no protection at all—if the hull and deck are really watertight. In practice there is almost certain to be some leakage somewhere, so an unprotected system can prove a short-life system. Even if dried out at the end of a days running, and hatches left open for ventilation, a hull atmosphere is usually a damp one.

External Wiring

All wiring external to the radio compartment should be cabled together and supported as high as possible in the hull. Receiver/servo wiring must *always* be kept separate from wires carrying current to other electrical components (e.g. the propulsion motor or secondary servos). Thus if a particular servo, say a motor speed controller, is mounted outside the radio compartment, treat wiring to the receiver and radio separately and keep them separate. Never cable propulsion motor wiring and receiver/servo wiring together.

CHAPTER 5

RUDDER CONTROL

Rudder is the one *essential* control for operating model boats by remote control. However many additional functions are contemplated, rudder remains the first choice for primary control which must be given preference over any other control. This means that it should *always* be operated by its own servo. For similar reasons, rudder control should also be *proportional* (i.e. operated by a proportional servo).

This chapter is concerned primarilly with rudders for power boats, although many aspects—particularly balancing and rudder movement required—apply equally well to yachts. Yacht rudders, however, are subject to further description in Chapter 9.

The turning power required from a rudder—as given by its size and its movement to one side or the other—is difficult to estimate. It depends to a large extent on the type and size of the boat, and even more so on the boat's speed. Slow boats need fairly large rudder areas to be effective. Faster planing hulls need progressively smaller rudder areas to avoid being 'overturned' by rudder response at high speeds. So much smaller, in fact, that they may be relatively ineffective at low speeds.

Rudder Movement

Starting first with rudder *movement,* here requirements are fairly specific. Regardless of the size of rudder and speed of the boat, a rudder movement greater than 30 degrees either way is excessive. It

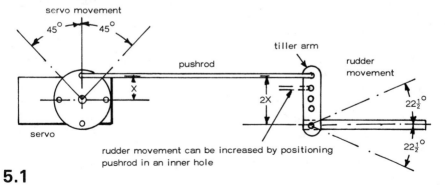

5.1

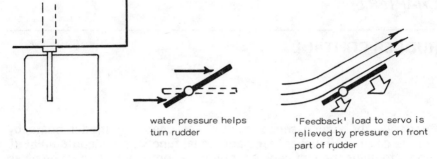

water pressure helps
turn rudder

'Feedback' load to servo is
relieved by pressure on front
part of rudder

5.2

will not improve steering response, more likely making it less effective. Excessive rudder movement will only produce a lot of drag, slowing the boat down, and *reduce* turning effort because the water flow past the rudder is stalled.

This leads to the simple rule that the length of a tiller arm needs to be twice the lever arm movement of a conventional servo—Fig. 5.1. Since the servo movement is typically 45 degrees either side of centre, this will give a rudder movement $22\frac{1}{2}$ degrees either side of the centre, which should be enough. If more rudder movement is found to be desirable, then alternative hole positions can be provided along the tiller arm for trial-and-error positioning of the pushrod for greater rudder movement.

Balanced Rudders

Conventional servos usually have enough push-pull power to operate rudders on most powerboats, except for larger models. With large yachts (M class or bigger), they will not be powerful enough unless the rudder is *balanced.* Balanced rudders are to be preferred on all types and sizes of powerboats, too, because they generally reduce the load on the servo, which in consequence operates on less current and prolongs the battery life.

Balancing a rudder is simply a matter of positioning the hinge line back from the leading edge so that part of the rudder area comes in front of the hinge line, and part behind it. When the rudder is turned, water pressure on the forward area then acts to assist rudder movement. When the rudder is *held* in a turned position water pressure on the front then acts to reduce the force necessary to hold this position against water pressure on the area behind the hinge line—Fig. 5.2.

If the areas in front and behind the hinge line are equal, the rudder is (apparently) fully balanced. Only small forces should be needed to turn it, and hold it any position. In fact, it would be over-balanced because

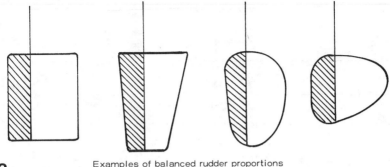

5.3 Examples of balanced rudder proportions

the forward area of a rudder develops more 'sideways' force than the after area. Thus a force would be needed to *stop* it from trying to continue turning once displaced from its central position.

The best balance is achieved when the forward area of the rudder is about one third of the total area—i.e. one third of the rudder area is in front of the hinge line and two thirds of the area is behind the hinge line—Fig. 5.3. This holds good regardless of the actual shape (or size) of the rudder; or whether it is to be used in a slow speed or high speed craft.

Increasing Rudder Efficiency

As a general rule a rudder will be most efficient when its area lies fully in the slipstream of the propeller. It does not really matter, though, if part of the rudder area does come above or below the slipstream. However, for the *same* rudder area, a high aspect ratio shape which comes well into the slipstream will be more effective than a short, stubby shape which does not—Fig. 5.4.

Rudder efficiency is only really important on high speed powerboats (and racing yachts). High efficiency means that a smaller area can be used to give the required turning power with less drag. On slower craft, any lack of turning power can be overcome by fitting a larger area rudder (not necessarily by increasing rudder movement for reasons explained earlier).

Rudder Trim

Pushrod length should be adjusted so that when the servo is in its neutral position the rudder is central. If the model does not run straight with this setting (e.g. due to propeller torque, or possibly slight asymmetry in the hull shape), then the transmitter trim control can be used to adjust the rudder as necessary. The trim control can then be left in this position. Some modellers prefer to re-adjust the servo push

53

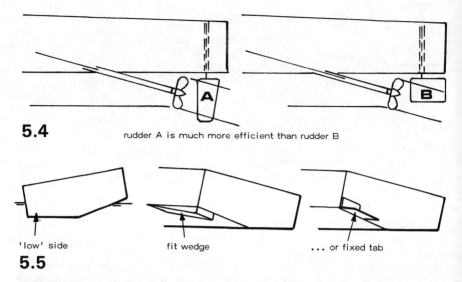

5.4   rudder A is much more efficient than rudder B

'low' side   fit wedge   ... or fixed tab

5.5

rod by trial and error to arrive at the required amount of rudder offset for straight running with the servo in the neutral position. This leaves the trim control available for 'fine' steering in either direction.

On fast powerboats (and racing yachts), permanent rudder offset (rudder trim) for straight steering with neutral rudder control position is often regarded as undesirable, because an offset rudder has more drag than a straight (centralised) one. On powerboats it is possible to trim for straight running with central rudder by fitting an offset trim tab (or differential adjustment of transom flaps, if fitted); or a small wedge on the 'low' side of the hull—Fig. 5.5. The tab is bent down, or the wedge

Balanced moderately high aspect ratio rudders are best for power boats. Typical proprietary range by Ripmax in different sizes.

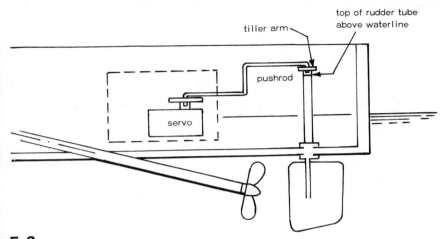

tiller arm

top of rudder tube above waterline

pushrod

servo

5.6

trimmed to shape, by trial-and-error to generate the required amount of lift to offset torque, tending to roll and turn the boat to one side. Complete correction is, of course, only obtainable at one particular speed.

In the case of a racing yacht, unless the hull lines are slightly asymmetrical, (or the keel out of line), adjusting the mast position fore-and-aft can eliminate the tendency for the model to turn to one side or another when sailing with a neutral rudder position. If the yacht persistently tries to turn into the wind, then this can usually be cured by moving the mast aft. If the yacht persistently tries to turn away from the wind, moving the mast forward can effect a cure. It is far more important to trim a racing yacht for straight running' via mast positioning than it is to apply corrective measures to a powerboat to ensure that it runs straight when the rudder is straight.

Installation Notes

Powerboat rudders consist of a blade mounted on a spindle for the rudder stock, running in a tube. The tube is often flanged and threaded so that it can be bolted' in place through a hole in the hull bottom. Unless specifically called for—e.g. in a scale model—the rudder tube should terminate inside the hull, but well above the water line—Fig. 5.6. The tiller arm then simply attaches to the top of the rudder spindle for simple coupling to the rudder servo via a pushrod or snake.

Where possible the deck section over the tiller area should be made accessible—e.g. come under the main hatch covering the radio installation, or under a separate, tightly sealed hatch in the deck. This will give access to the whole rudder assembly should it ever need attention.

The most likely cause of trouble is corrosion. For that reason, rudder blade and rudder tube should be in brass, with the rudder spindle also in brass, or stainless steel for greater strength. Stainless steel and brass are not good metals to have in contact in salt water, however, and a stainless steel rudder and spindle would be a preferred selection.

Metal-to-metal rubbing connection should be avoided on the servo linkage, as previously noted (Chapter 3). However, the fact that a metal rudder spindle rubs in a metal rudder tube does not matter. This part is effectively 'earthed' by immersion in water and will not generate electrical 'noise'.

Steering without Rudder

The original statement that rudder is an essential control holds good, despite this sub-title. But there are occasions where rudder may not give all the control desirable for close manoeuvering at low speeds. Not a great deal can be done about this with single screw powerboats, but with twin screw electric powered installations it can be a different matter.

To be fully effective for slower speed manoeuvering, twin-screw installations should be opposite hand – preferably a left hand propeller on the port shaft and a right hand propeller on the starboard shaft. It must also be possible to control each propulsion motor independently, i.e. use one servo for speed control on each motor.

It will then be found quite easy to steer the model at lower speeds by adjusting engine speeds. But the real advantage comes when manoeuvering and docking. With independent engine control and opposite hand props it should be easy, with practice, to turn the boat in its own length (one engine ahead, the other astern).

CHAPTER 6

I/C ENGINE CONTROL

Engines specifically developed or adapted for radio control have a throttle-type carburettor invariably operated by lever movement—Fig. 6.1. Throttling range is from fully open (maximum speed) to nearly closed (idling speed). The latter position of the lever is adjustable via a stop.

Throttled versions of both glow motors and diesels are available. As a general rule glow motors have a much more flexible throttle response than diesels, a wider operating range and a lower (and smoother) idling speed. A wide speed range is of less significance with boats than aircraft since there is less call to operate powerboats at intermediate speeds. Where speed performance is the main aim, however, the higher running speeds and higher force output for a given size favours the choice of a glow motor. Also glow motors generally produce less vibration when running than diesels. Vibration can be a cause of trouble through 'fatigue' of soldered connections, etc, and even affect modern solid state electrical components. (Vibration troubles were, of course, very much worse in the days when radio control systems used valves, relays and reed banks).

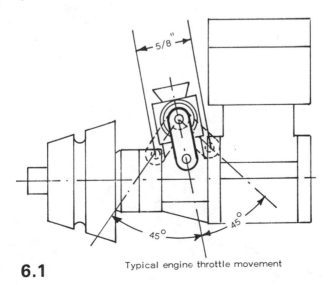

6.1   Typical engine throttle movement

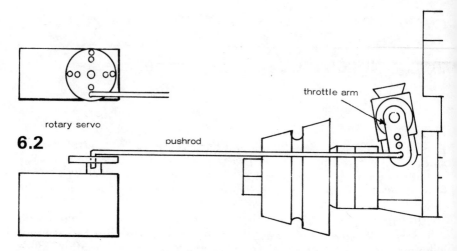

rotary servo

6.2

pushrod

throttle arm

Connecting up a throttle control is basically very simple. All it needs is a rigid push rod connecting the servo output to the throttle arm—Fig. 4.2. The typical push-pull travel of a conventional servo is about $\frac{5}{8}$ inch (see also Chapter 3). Throttle levers are proportional to match so that 'full travel' of a push rod connected to the top hole in the throttle arm usually corresponds to full throttle movement. Alternative hole positions on both the throttle arm and a standard (rotary) servo output disc or arm enable different amounts of movement to be obtained if necessary by changing hole positions.

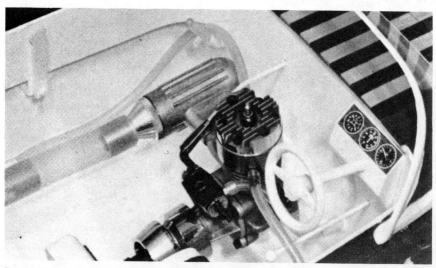

Throttle control operation via a snake. The engine is mounted in the cockpit in a scale speedboat type hull, with radio gear and servo under the foredeck.

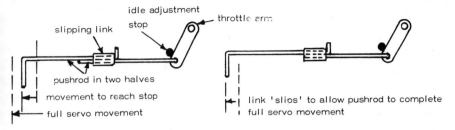

idle adjustment

slipping link stop throttle arm

pushrod in two halves

|← movement to reach stop

|← full servo movement

link 'slips' to allow pushrod to complete full servo movement

6.3

It is important that servo movement and throttle arm movement should match. If, for example, the push-pull movement given by the servo is greater than the available throttle arm movement the servo will reach a stalled condition at one or both end(s) of the movement. Since throttle position is selected by a ratchet-braked (transmitter) stick, it will then *remain* in this stalled position, considerably overloading the receiver battery and even damaging the servo circuitry.

This possibility can be overcome by incorporating a *slip link* in the push rod. The simplest type of slip link is a short piece of tight-fitting silicon rubber tube. The push rod is made in two pieces, each slipped through the tube and the ends turned up as shown in Fig. 6.3. If, however, the pushrod movement comes up against a mechanical stop (i.e. at the end(s) of the throttle arm movement), the joint in the push rod will slip and allow the servo movement to continue to full travel and switch itself off. Some other simple types of 'flexible' throttle links are shown in Fig. 6.4.

Basically, there should be no need to use a flexible link in the throttle push rod, with the (alternative holes) adjustment available on the throttle arm and servo output. It is a fairly simple matter to synchronise the movements so that full pushrod travel equals full throttle arm travel. The idling speed position is more important to set up properly, since the actual throttle position here is set by the idling screw stop adjustment. If the extreme movements of the servo are matched to this, then full throttle position leaves some tolerance, i.e. the pushrod movement can be very slightly less than the *full* throttle movement available with little or no effect on actual maximum speed resulting.

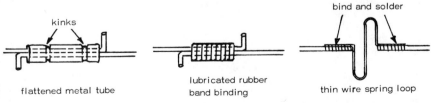

kinks

flattened metal tube

lubricated rubber band binding

bind and solder

thin wire spring loop

6.4

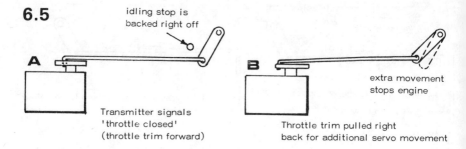

6.5

idling stop is
backed right off

A

Transmitter signals
'throttle closed'
(throttle trim forward)

B

extra movement
stops engine

Throttle trim pulled right
back for additional servo movement

Many modellers prefer to take matching servo movement and throttle movement one stage further. The (transmitter) throttle control is invariably associated with a separate 'trim' control. This is backed off to the full forward position. The pushrod length is then adjusted so that when throttle closed is signalled by the transmitter stick the throttle is moved to its correct idling position, as established by the setting of the idling screw stop on the throttle. This idling screw is then backed right off.

The (transmitter) throttle stick will then give a throttling range from idling to full throttle, and is used normally in this manner. The system now, however, also has the ability to stop the engine when required. Simply move the (transmitter) throttle stick to the idling position, then move the *trim* control downwards. This will give a small further movement of the throttle arm past its idling position to stop the engine—Fig. 6.5.

Installation Notes

Marine engines are mounted back-to-front by comparison with their aircraft counterparts, i.e. with the flywheel aft and the whole engine

Trim movement associated with the throttle control can be adjusted to stop an i/c engine, as explained in the test.

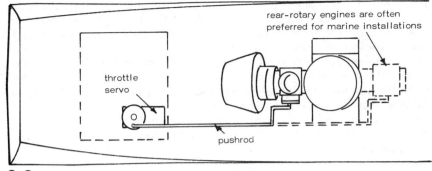

rear-rotary engines are often preferred for marine installations

throttle servo

pushrod

6.6

tilted downwards to line up with the propeller shaft. Engine position is usually around midships, with the radio installation aft of it.

This can present a problem in that the throttle push rod for straightforward installation must pass over or alongside the flywheel-Fig. 6.6.—where it may get in the way of, or be bent by, the leather thong looped round the flywheel to start the engine. It is best to avoid this if possible, even if the pushrod is taken over the centre of the flywheel where it is least likely to be fouled by the starting cord.

Possible alternatives are shown in Fig. 6.7. Diagram A uses a snake instead of a rigid pushrod to connect servo to throttle arm. The snake is taken in any easy bend, as far forward as necessary, to double back onto the throttle arm, clamping the outer at suitable points to prevent whipping.

Although this calls for a relatively long length of snake, friction should still be negligible using a snake instead of a rigid pushrod to connect servo to throttle arm with a PTFE outer tube or tube liner.

Method B is more direct mechanically and may be preferred. It merely carries the pushrod well to one side past the flywheel position where it connects to a simple paralleling movement. This is simply a stirrup bent from wire with a brass tube hinge. A second short pushrod then connects the other arm of the stirrup to the throttle arm. The only real disadvantages of this hook-up is that it has three pivot joints in the

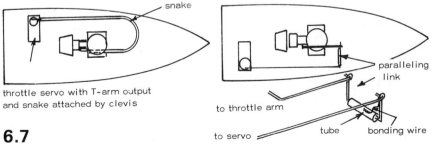

snake

throttle servo with T-arm output and snake attached by clevis

paralleling link

to throttle arm

to servo

tube

bonding wire

6.7

run instead of just one with the possibility of introducing more free play and electrical 'noise'. Soldering a length of flexible wire between the brass tube and the wire stirrup will eliminate 'noise' being generated between these two metal components.

The simplest solution of all, of course, is to mount the throttle servo forward of the engine on its own, where it can connect directly to the engine throttle arm. On larger powerboats it may be possible (and even desirable from the weight distribution point of view) to mount the complete radio installation forward of the engine. In this case the *rudder* pushrod may well require displacing sideways to run well clear of the flywheel.

CHAPTER 7

ELECTRIC MOTOR CONTROLS

The best method of providing propulsion motor control is via a proprietary speed controller. There are two main types.

(i) The all-electric speed controller which takes the place of the (second) servo and works directly from the receiver with propulsion motor battery connected to motor through the servo.

(ii) A separate speed controller which itself is operated by a conventional servo, i.e. this system requires both a (second) servo *and* a controller unit. The controller itself may be electro-mechanical (e.g. potentiometer type), or again based on electronic circuity.

Either type is usually designed to provide on-off switching plus infinitely variable speeds forward and astern (reverse). Performance is limited only by their wattage rating—i.e. they cannot be used for controlling electric motors of higher wattage rating than their specified rating. Their main disadvantage is that both types are relatively expensive, which could make speed control the most costly part of the installation. Either system is also bulkier and heavier than a conven-

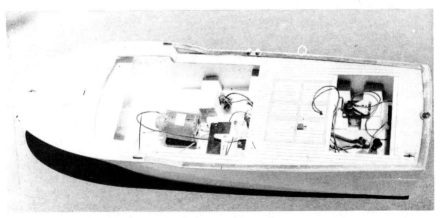

Even small hard chine hulls can provide plenty of room for installing radio control. Second servo for motor, switching would have been better located in aft compartment.

Ready-to-go radio controlled electric powered boats (and cars) are basically toy shop lines. Scope is. limited. A modeller can get far better performance by fitting out his own model.

tional servo, but this is unlikely to be a particular problem other than in smaller models.

Alternative methods of electric motor control can be derived by mechanical switching, using a conventional servo to generate the necessary movements, although the extent of control available is more limited. Also switching contacts can be unreliable when operating in unfavourable environments (e.g. salt water atmosphere). Thus fully enclosed switches (e.g. microswitches) are to be preferred to open contacts in such switching systems.

The simplest system of all is to use a conventional servo as a 'throttle' servo, i.e. controlled by a braked transmitter stick, to operate an ordinary switch for on-off switching—Fig. 7.1. This is an expensive way of getting a very basic control response, which can be done just as

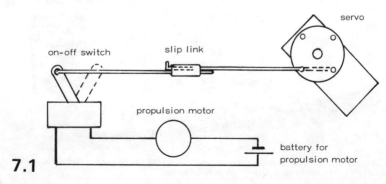

7.1

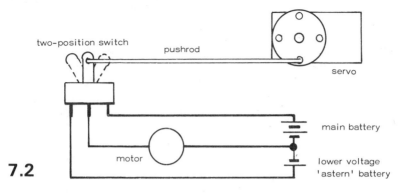

two-position switch

pushrod

servo

main battery

motor

lower voltage
'astern' battery

7.2

well manually at the start and end of a run. Also it is not *quite* as simple as it appears. A 'slip' link or 'flexible' link will be necessary in the pushrod connecting servo to switch arm (or slide) to ensure that the servo is not stalled at the completion of switch movement. (See Chapter 6).

By using a two-position switch and *two* batteries, this direct method of switch operation can provide forward-stop-reverse control selection—Fig. 7.2. A refinement to this circuit is to use a lower voltage for one battery to give reduced speed astern. A further possibility is to use a double-pole changeover switch, or two separate switches, to provide ahead-astern working from a single battery.

Practical control circuits of this type would normally use *microswitches* positioned so that they can be operated directly from a T-arm output of a rotary servo. Fig. 7.3. shows a suitable circuit, using two switches, giving stop-start-ahead-astern from a single battery. Reduced running speed astern can be provided by inserting a resistance in the 'astern' circuit, as shown. The resistance in this case could be about the same as the nominal resistance of the electric motor—e.g. typically 10 or 15 ohms. The wattage rating of the resistor should be at least equal to that of the motor.

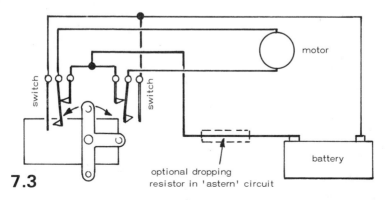

motor

switch

switch

battery

7.3

optional dropping
resistor in 'astern' circuit

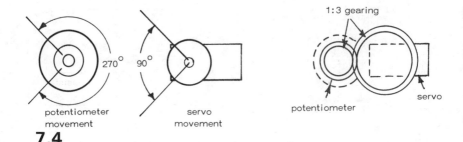

potentiometer
movement

servo
movement

1:3 gearing

potentiometer

servo

7.4

Potentiometer Speed Controls

The simplest type of speed controller for an electric motor is a potentiometer providing a variable resistance in the motor circuit. A practical difficulty then arises in that the usual (full) movement of a (rotary) potentiometer is 270 degrees and that of a servo only about 90 degrees. Thus without movement multiplication, only one third of the potentiometer range will be available—Fig. 7.4. And even with movement multiplication from a rotary servo outfit, maximum practical full movement is still less than 180 degrees unless a direct gear drive is used between the two. Some smaller types of circular potentiometers are designed with only 60° rotary movement covering the full track. Unfortunately these are only usually produced with low power rating—i.e. typically $\frac{1}{4}$ watt.

Basically, therefore, an *in-line* potentiometer is needed for direct operation by a servo, rather than the more familiar circular type. Linkage can then be adjusted to provide full potentiometer range from the limited output movement available from either a rotary or linear servo.

If the potentiometer is of a type which has an 'off' position at one end of the track, it can also provide on-off switching.

The main disadvantage of any potentiometer control is that it is wasteful of battery power, although this is not usually serious, particularly if low resistance potentiometer is used to give a smoother, less drastic, change of speed with potentiometer movement. The main limitations are practical requirements, particularly when using potentiometers in relatively high current circuits.

The more common *carbon track* potentiometers usually have a low wattage rating (usually less than 1 watt) and are unlikely to be available in resistance valves less than 100 ohms. Unfortunately most compact in-line potentiometers are of this type. *Wire-wound* potentiometers have a higher power rating, usually up to 3 watts continuous rating, and are available in resistance from 10 ohms upwards in logarithmic 'steps' (e.g. 22 ohms, 47 ohms, 100 ohms, 220 ohms, etc).

66

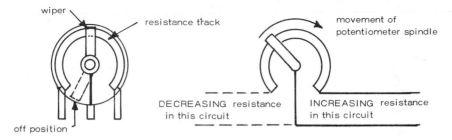

Potentiometers may also be of *linear* or *logarithmic* type. A linear potentiometer is best for speed control since the resistance charge is directly proportional to movement. A *logarithmic* potentiometer produces an increasing greater change in resistance with spindle movement.

Where a circular potentiometer is used incorporating an 'off' position, wiring connections are important. A conventional (rotary) potentiometer has three terminals, connection being made to the central tag and one end tag. Connecting up the 'wrong' way round will result in 'stop' (the off position) following on from maximum speed rather than minimum speed. Thus logically the potentiometer must be connected up to its 'clockwise' tag and central tag so that when turned from the 'off' position in a clockwise direction track resistance decreases gradually from maximum to zero. Fig. 7.5. should make this point clear.

Stop-Start with a Potentiometer

If a potentiometer of suitable rating cannot be found with an 'off' position, then stop-start can easily be added by positioning a microswitch near the limit of the 'slow' movement. This switch is then wired into the motor circuit to provide a positive switch-off when the potentiometer is moved to this position—Fig. 7.6.

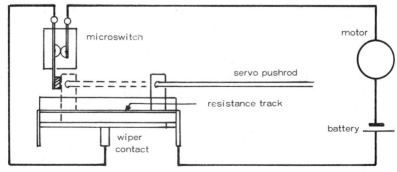

7.6

67

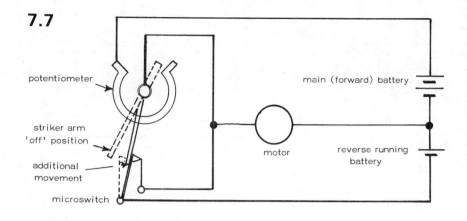

7.7

Astern with Potentiometer Control

Provided the potentiometer has a built-in 'off' position it is possible also to provide 'astern' via a microswitch operated by movement of the trim control associated with the main transmitter control (see also the following section on Saving a Servo). Such a system is shown in Fig. 7.7. When the servo is moved past its 'stop' position by operation of trim, the movement operates the microswitch to close the 'astern' circuit connecting the second battery to the motor with reverse polarity. The main battery remains isolated through the 'off' position on the potentiometer.

Proportional speed controller for electric motors. This replaces a servo for motor control and is capable of providing infinitely variable speed from stop to full ahead or full astern. Electronic controllers of this type are expensive and can only be used within their rated capacity (in this case 240 watts maximum output).

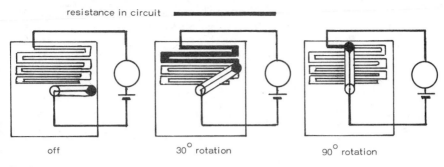

resistance in circuit ▬▬▬▬▬▬

off   30° rotation   90° rotation

7.8

The difficulty in achieving this extension of control is that there is normally a definite mechanical stop incorporated in the potentiometer preventing movement of the spindle past the off position. If this is not removable (and most potentiometers are integral units which cannot be disassembled readily without damage), the necessary extra movement can be obtained via a slipping clutch connecting the potentiometer drive to the potentiometer spindle. This will allow the striker arm to over-ride the 'stop' position movement, but pick up positively when movement is reversed past the stop position again.

Printed Circuit Potentiometer

A printed circuit potentiometer provides a better method of speed control than a conventional potentiometer since it can be 'tailored' to meet specific requirements, as well as providing straightforward-stop-reverse control. In this case the resistance element is usually of rectangular form. The principle of working is shown in Fig. 7.8. In the 'off' position the wiper arm is clear of the resistor strip, breaking the circuit. Initial movement of the wiper arm then brings the whole length of the resistor strip into the circuit. Further rotation of the wiper arm progressively decreases the length of resistor strip in circuit (and thus progressively decreases resistance) until after 90 degrees rotation only a minimal length of resistor strip remains in the circuit. Reversing the direction of the wiper arm progressively increases resistance in circuit until it eventually runs off the track and breaks the circuit.

As drawn in this diagram, only one half of the board is used. The other half can equally well have a similar resistance track swept by a second wiper (i.e. a two-arm wiper with separate connections). These can be connected up to give speed control in both forward and reverse directions, with a central 'off' position. Resistance foil area can be chosen both from the point of view of resistance required and current to be carried, and the pattern also designed to give linear resistance characteristics.

This form of custom-made potentiometer is known as a *control board*. It can be designed to fit directly on top of a rotary output servo with the two brushes mounted on the ends of a standard T-shaped servo output arm. Alternatively the board can be mounted separately and the brush arm driven directly by a pushrod connected to the servo—Fig. 7.9.

Limitations of Potentiometer Speed Controllers

Potentiometer-type speed controllers rely on rubbing contact between resistance track and brush (or brushes). They operate reliably only as long as the contact surfaces are clean. This is not necessarily a particular problem since printed circuit boards are readily accessible for cleaning when necessary; and can also readily be accommodated inside an airtight/watertight container along with the rest of the radio gear (see Chapter 4). If exposed, however, and operated in unfavourable atmospheres, the surface of the resistance element may suffer corrosion which will not necessarily 'wipe clean', especially if the unit has been idle for some time. Aluminium is probably better than copper in this respect for the resistance element; but a cadmium plated surface could be better still (Chapter 14).

With a conventional potentiometer, track and brush materials have to be accepted 'as made'. Since such components are produced for normally dry ambients, corrosion problems can arise when used for boat work.

One limitation common to all types of potentiometer speed controls is that they cannot be used for reversing wound field motors without additional (external) switching being incorporated in the circuit. Thus whilst it is easy enough to design a printed circuit potentiometer to provide two separate tracks for current reversal, this will only give speed control with the *same* direction of rotation with field wound motors.

Saving a Servo

This method of switch control can be operated by a servo already used for another control but utilising 'trim' movements of that servo. Normal movement of the servo, with 'trim' in the central position, does

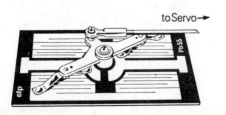

7.9

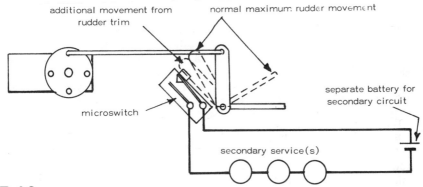

additional movement from rudder trim

normal maximum rudder movement

separate battery for secondary circuit

microswitch

secondary service(s)

7.10

not reach the switch positions. At any extreme position of the servo, however, operation of the trim control in the same direction produces extra movement of the servo arm to activate that switch—Fig. 7.10.

Realistically, this is only suitable for operating secondary controls, or over-riding a main control. It also must be 'safe' or acceptable, at its extreme position. This serverely limits the application of trim-movement switching.

For example, suppose the servo used controls rudder. Any additional servos operated by trim-movement switching would just mean that the rudder position would either have to be full left or full right. This would not be acceptable with the boat under way. Thus a separate servo (or controller) would be needed for propulsion motor speed control. A logical sequence of operation could then be:

(i)   Stop engine via the separate motor controller.

(ii)   Move rudder to say, full left using normal rudder control movement.

(iii)   Apply 'left trim' to rudder to activate microswitch A, which could then switch on one secondary service—e.g. switch on lights, or let go anchor, etc.

If this service is wired to operate through a *changeover* switch, then it will remain in operation when the servo is backed off; and be switched off by returning the servo to full movement again, plus trim. This would be a logical choice for operating navigation lights and similar 'static' services. For services requiring short term operation (e.g. winching), then straightforward *on-off* switching would be used. The service is then switched off by taking off 'trim'. In the first case there is an immediate release of the servo involved for use in its normal mode. In the second case, the servo is not available for use in its normal mode until the secondary service is no longer required to be operated (i.e. can be switched off).

Utilisation of limit switching can be done at both ends of the servo travel. Essentially, however, any such system still needs two servos for the main functional controls (i.e. rudder and engine).

Exactly the same principle of operating a switch by trim movement can be used to over-ride a main control. The most usual case is where a servo-operated speed controller which absorbs appreciable current is used for electric propulsion motor control, so that the full battery current is not available even in the maximum speed position. In this case the trim-operated switch is located at the 'ahead' end of the servo movement and used to bypass the battery current direct to the motor to give maximum possible motor speed.

CHAPTER 8

SECONDARY SERVICES

Any control which is not directly concerned with the handling of a motor boat is described as a secondary service. This is usually a 'working' feature added to a scale model, choice being in character with the craft and the individual modeller's ambitions in this respect. Theoretically, at least, this opens up possibilities for reproducing all full size working features—gun turrets that traverse, range and fire; Aldis lamp signalling; dropping depth charges, etc, on a naval craft for example; working water-cannon on firefighting ships; launching and recovery of rescue craft (the smaller craft also being radio controlled); cargo ships with working derricks; and so on. Realisation of a scale modeller's dream, in fact, limited only by the time and money he is prepared to spend on the project, and his ingenuity in creating such service in practical working form.

The first point to consider is how to operate these services.

Secondary working feature on this scale model fire-fighting ship is working water jets fed by a small electric motor powered pump with on-off switching via a third radio channel. The other two channels are used for steering and motor speed control.

Examples of fully detailed radio controlled scale ships. Models like this need to be large to accommodate all detail.

Mechanised movements can be operated directly (through linkages) by servos, but the conventional self-centering servo will only provide two one-way movements with proportional response—Fig. 8.1. It is also expensive to use additional servos in this way as each servo added requires an extra radio channel to operate it. But with expense no object and 8-, 10- or even 12-channel radio the logical choice, all these extra channels would be available for operating individual secondary services with their own servo, (or special servo as the case may be). A sail winch would be equally suitable for anchor winching, for example.

More realistically, as far as the majority of modellers are concerned, it is desirable to limit the number of extra channels required, and the number of additional servos. A single (extra) servo, for example, could

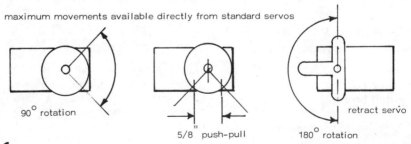

maximum movements available directly from standard servos

90° rotation

5/8" push-pull

retract servo

180° rotation

8.1

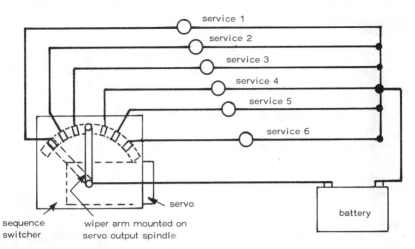

service 1
service 2
service 3
service 4
service 5
service 6
servo
battery
sequence switcher
wiper arm mounted on servo output spindle

8.2

be used to drive a sequence switch, as shown diagramatically in Fig. 8.2. From its neutral 'off' position, it can be moved to position 1, 2, 3 in sequence one way; or positions 4, 5, 6 in sequence the other way, giving six separate switched circuits.

As an example, considering the six switched services offered by Fig. 8.2, allocation could be:—

(a) **'Left hand' movement**

    (1)   Navigation lights on

    (2)   Searchlight on

    (3)   Horn or siren on

    Position (2) could be paralleled with position (1).

(b) **Central position of servo**—all secondary services off

(c) **'Right hand' movement**

    (4)   Gun turret traverses (via electric motor drive)

    (5)   Guns elevate (via solenoid or another small electric motor)

    (6)   Guns 'fire' (e.g. triggered 'clapper')

    This system is shown in diagramatical form again in Fig. 8.3.

Any particular service is then selected by appropriate movement of the Tx control stick to make the servo movement and corresponding switch brush movement 'dwell' in the appropriate position. If the stick is ratchet braked (i.e. a normal throttle control stick), the stick can then be released. If not, it will have to be held in that position for as long as the servo is required. In either case only one secondary service circuit can be selected at a time, and it may have to be switched momentarily

Naval ships are a very popular subject for radio control and can achieve a high level of realism.

through other services to reach the required position. This calls for ingenuity in the allocation of switching positions; and, if necessary, in paralleling switching positions to obtain simultaneous operation of two appropriate secondary services.

This method is a basic approach, with obvious limitations. However, it is fairly straightforward to design, and suitable simple contact patterns can readily be produced in printed circuit boards.

The most obvious limitation is the speed at which a standard servo

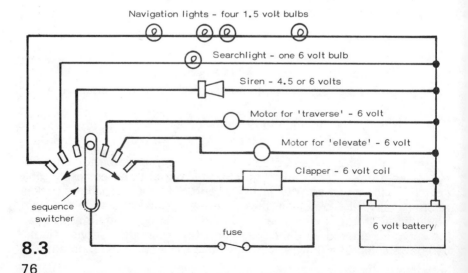

8.3

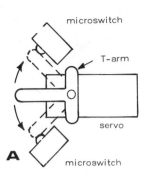

microswitch

T-arm

servo

A

microswitch

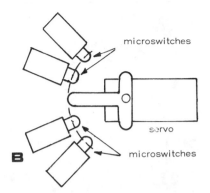

microswitches

servo

B

microswitches

8.4

operates. 'Full' positioning—position 3 or 6 on the above illustrations —would be reached in a quarter of a second or less. This means that a braked Tx stick is virtually essential for practical selection of intermediate positions, and even then they have to be established by 'estimated' stick positions—e.g. one third, two thirds and respectively. Also the design of the switcher should be such that the wiper arm does not bridge adjacent contacts. Yet it can prove to be a workable system.

An alternative approach is to use a servo to operate switches at the limits of its movement. This provides *positive* selection of two (switched) services, one at each end of the servo movement. It is, in fact, identical in principle to the systems used for electric motor control, described in Chapter 7.

There are several ways in which such switching systems can be rigged. In all cases it is best to operate the servo from a ratched-braked transmitter stick so that the Tx stick can be released when a 'switched' position is selected.

A model like this can take years to complete — possibly being operated as a relatively 'bare' model first and then being added to over the following years.

More fine example of extremely realistic radio controlled scale ships.

In Fig. 8.4A a switch (preferably a microswitch) is located at each end of the servo output movement. Moving the Tx stick to its full movement one way then makes the servo respond to operate one switch, which is held operated as long as the Tx stick remains in the position to which it is moved. Once the Tx stick is backed off, the servo is switched off. Full movement of the Tx stick in the other direction operates the second switch to select the second servo directly.

In theory, at least, there is no reason why more switches could not be positioned at intermediate positions of the servo movement, as in Fig. 8.4B. Each could then switch its own secondary service. However, this has the same limitations as the system previously described. An intermediate position (switch) is not positively selectable—the correct Tx stick position has to be established by trial-and-error. Also to select an end position switch will mean momentarily switching on an intermediate switch.

The switching facility provided will depend on the *type* of switch used at the switch positions. A straightforward off-on (normally off)

Single-pole
on-off

Double-pole
changeover

changeover

Two-circuit
changeover

Switch contact arrangements

8.5

switch will give on-off switching of that service. Alternatives are a *changeover* switch which works on an on-off-on-off-etc sequence basis; and a *double pole* switch which provides reversing facilities for a secondary servo operated by an electric motor—e.g. see Fig. 8.5. In this particular case, however, the electric motor would always be moving in one direction or another. There is no 'off' position provided by a single pole changeover switch.

Secondary services which are powered by an electric motor which has to be started and stopped are best controlled by introducing a limit switch in the output movement of the motor. This is simply another (on-off) micro switch activated by the movement itself reaching the limit of travel required—Fig. 8.6. (This is an identical switching circuit to that described for S.C.U.s in Chapter 10).

The points to check in the design of such switching circuits are:—

(i) That switching 'off' by a limit switch does not permanently leave the motor switched off when the first (servo operated) switch is released by returning the servo to neutral. In other words, this first switch should be of double-pole changeover type.

(ii) That the circuit loop closed by a limit switch does not short circuit the first switch, or the battery in that service.

Parallel & Series Circuits

Any one secondary *circuit* may include more than one working component in it. For example, one circuit using port, starboard, steaming and stern light bulbs. There is the possibility of connecting them each in *series* or *parallel*.

Series connection (Fig. 8.7A) saves wiring since only one wire has to be led from one side of the battery from bulb to bulb and back to the other side of the battery. The disadvantage of series connection is that

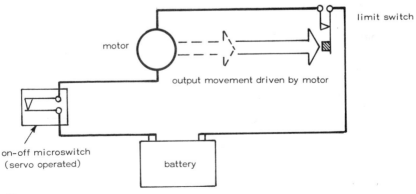

limit switch

motor

output movement driven by motor

on-off microswitch
(servo operated)

battery

8.6

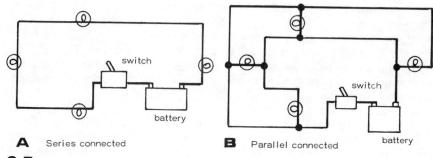

A   Series connected   **B**   Parallel connected

8.7

the voltage required from the battery is the *sum* of the voltage ratings of the bulbs—e.g. four 2.5 volt bulbs would equal $4 \times 2.5 = 10$ volts. Also, should one bulb fail, all the others will go out because the circuit is broken.

Parallel connection (Fig. 8.7B) means running two wires to each bulb, one of which goes to a 'common' battery terminal and the other to a 'common' terminal on the switch. Battery voltage required is then only the same as that of the rated bulb voltage, but with a higher current drain. Failure of one bulb will not affect working of the others.

The same principles apply if two separate circuits are selected simultaneously by switching. If the two circuits are then effectively in *series,* then there will be a drop in voltage (e.g. a searchlight switched into a navigation light circuit would result in dimming of all bulbs). If the two circuits are effectively in *parallel* then voltage will be maintained, but there will be extra current drain from the battery.

CHAPTER 9

YACHT CONTROLS

Whilst radio can be added to a free sailing yacht to convert it to radio control there are small, but important, differences between the design of a free sailing yacht and one planned for radio from the start. The first is a matter of access to the interior of the hull. The hatch opening on a radio controlled design is made larger to facilitate installation of the radio gear; and reach it for battery charging, removal of gear for checking, laying up, etc. Also more attention must be paid to detail design to ensure completely watertight topsides as far as possible, placing a premium on the hatch seal, 'leakproofing' of any through-deck openings (e.g. through which sheet hauling lines pass), and elimination of any unnecessary deck openings. For example, on a radio control yacht (or any other type of sailing craft), the mast(s) should always be stepped on the deck, not passed through the deck and stepped on the hog or keelson.

Hatch design is particularly important. Flush-fitting hatches are

Radio control for racing class yachts is the 'complete' answer. It has rendered vane steering obsolete.

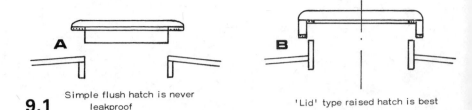

9.1

Simple flush hatch is never leakproof

'Lid' type raised hatch is best

difficult (but not impossible) to seal. A raised hatch surround is to be preferred, with the hatch itself fitting like a 'tin can' lid—Fig. 9.1. This enables the seal to be placed above rather than in line with the potential water entry passage and makes this passage itself self-draining. Secondary sealing strips can also be used to keep this passage dry.

For the seals to be fully effective they need to be held under compression when the hatch is fitted. Rubber band tension—good enough on a free sailing yacht—is not satisfactory. The most positive way of closing the hatch is to *screw* it in place—Fig. 9.2 Tedious, perhaps, to have to unscrew it again at the end of the day for access to the battery for charging (and then leaving it off for ventilation). But certainly the most reliable method of tight sealing. Also if the hatch top is in Perspex, it is always possible to see that 'all is well' inside the hull even when the hatch is screwed in place.

The other main difference in the design of a free sailing yacht and a radio control yacht is in the type and fixing of the rudder used. On free sailing yachts the rudder is usually front hinged to a skeg, or perhaps directly to the trailing edge of the keel—Fig. 9.3A. This produces an *unbalanced* rudder which could require quite high servo power to operate on a large yacht adapted to radio control. If specifically designed for radio control from the start, a balanced rudder is much to be preferred, where the hinge line is set about one-third back along the rudder. This can be done by fitting extended hinge plates or rudder hangings to the skeg (or keel)—Fig. 9.3B.—but the rudder stock still has to enter the hull through a tube at the hinge line position. It is thus

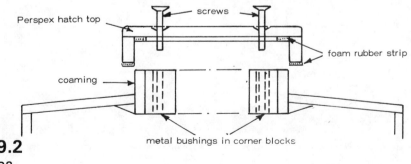

Perspex hatch top · screws · foam rubber strip · coaming · metal bushings in corner blocks

9.2

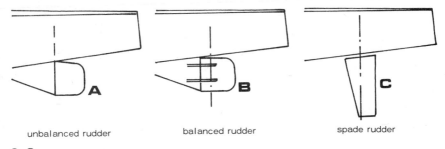

unbalanced rudder   balanced rudder   spade rudder

9.3

simpler to use the stock and tube as a hinge. The value of the skeg is then debatable and it can conveniently be eliminated in favour of using what is generally known as a *spade* rudder on its own—Fig. 9.3C.

The most efficient form of spade rudder is one which is deeper than its breadth, hinged at mid-cord at its upper line, but with the leading edge swept back to give a bottom cord about one half the top cord. This will give powerful rudder action with balanced proportions, greatly reducing the servo power required to operate it. The trailing edge may also be swept back slightly, bringing the leading edge of the bottom of the rudder slightly behind the hinge line. Whatever the proportions used, the hinge line position should be such that not less than 30 per cent and not more than 40 per cent of the rudder area comes in front of the hinge line.

Sail Setting Requirements

Sail setting by radio control is done by a sail winch or similar sail control unit (generally known as a S.C.U.) capable of producing a sheet-hauling movement. Normally both the jib sheet and the mainsail sheet are hauled together by the same winch. Running rigging is therefore different to that of a free sailing yacht, but this still does not dispense with the need for conventional bowsie adjustment of the two sails—Fig. 9.4. Manual adjustment allows the sails to be set differentially for initial trimming.

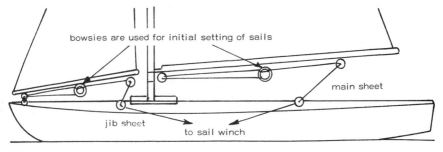

bowsies are used for initial setting of sails

main sheet

jib sheet

to sail winch

9.4

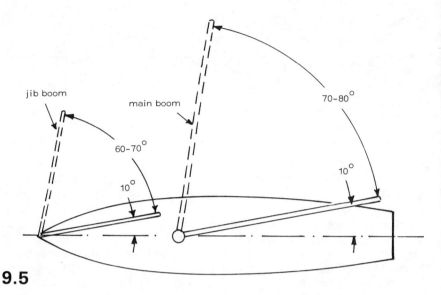

9.5

Sheet *travel* required from the sail winch or S.C.U. can be worked out from the basic requirement that the movement required on the main boom is from 10 degrees relative to the centreline in the extreme close-hauled position, to 80-90 degrees for running—Fig. 9.5. A 90 degree boom angle is not necessary, and the boom will usually foul the shroud before this anyway. Jib boom movement can be similar, although again an extreme position of 90 degrees is not required, nor desirable.

The above needs a little qualification. The sheet travel to give sail setting adjustment from 10 degrees to 80–90 degrees applies only when you aim to sail a full range of courses from beat through reach to a run purely under remote control. (In that case it is also possible, theoretically at least, to dispense with manual adjustment via bowsies entirely, although in practice this would still be desirable for initial setting up of sheet lengths). If it is only intended to sail a single course

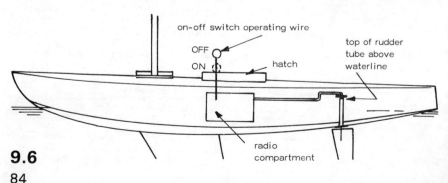

9.6

at any one time—e.g. a run *or* a reach *or* a beat, a much smaller sheet travel is required. The sails are then re-set by manual adjustment at the end of one course to sail another course, and further adjusted by radio control as necessary when actually sailing that course.

Installation Details

Logically the complete radio installation—receiver, battery and servos—should be grouped together, mounted in a watertight box

The non-class yacht, sailed for fun, can give very rewarding results on just 1-function (rudder) control and prove quite inexpensive to fit out.

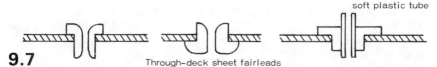

soft plastic tube

9.7 Through-deck sheet fairleads

immediately under the hatch position where everything is most accessible—Fig. 9.6. This should present no particular problems although it may be preferable in many cases to mount the sail winch or S.C.U. separately (outside the radio 'compartment'). A choice also has to be made whether the sail winch or S.C.U. is installed completely below the deck with just the sheet lines emerging through the deck; or with the 'working' part of the S.C.U. (the winch drum or lever) above deck.

In the former case sheets need to be taken through 'leakproof' fairleads or plastic grommets similar to Fig. 9.7. The best type of material is PTFE because of its low friction, which means that the grommet can have a minimal clearance on the hole for the sheet. Nylon bushes are also satisfactory, but need more generous hole clearnace and well rounded ends to the hole to prevent chafing. Metal bushings or rubber grommets are *not* suitable. Each fairlead will inevitably be a source of drip leakage and so should be positioned well away from radio gear.

If the sheet hauling mechanism is mounted above deck, only one leakage point needs to be sealed—the hole through which the driving spindle emerges. This can be sealed with a loose fitting O-ring coated with waterproof grease. On the whole, therefore, an above-deck winch drum or lever can produce a more watertight installation. However such a layout is more vulnerable than one where all working elements are below deck.

Other points to consider for 'watertightness' are the rudder tube and radio receiver on-off switch. The rudder tube should terminate inside the hull as high as possible, making sure that its top is above the waterline. There is no real advantage in carrying it through to the deck with the tiller arm above deck as this would need a deck opening for the pushrod connecting the servo to the tiller. Also, again, the tiller mechanism is in a more vulnerable position. However a 'hidden' tiller position can cause difficulties if it needs servicing—e.g. if corrosion has caused binding which really calls for removal of the tiller arm and withdrawal of the rudder to deal with.

Where the hatch is secured with screws, an extension to the receiver on-off switch virtually becomes essential. If the switch is mounted vertically, a wire arm fitted through a hole drilled in the switch movement can be used, emerging through the top of the hatch via a tight fitting rubber seal or tiny gaiter. Bend the top of the arm into a full loop and arrange the switch that pushing the arm *down* switches 'on'.

The Receiver Aerial

The receiver aerial can be something of a problem. It is often possible to get away with looping the aerial wire around the front of the hull well away from the servo(s) taped to the underside of the deck—Fig. 9.8, position A.

This will, however, greatly reduce range and may not give the radio performance required. Taking the aerial wire through the deck and then up to a suitable point on the mast or a shroud (position B); or better still the backstay (position C); is much better and easy to disconnect if secured in position with a rubber band looped over a small hook. This again can cause problems at times if the standing rigging is stainless steel wire rather than cord.

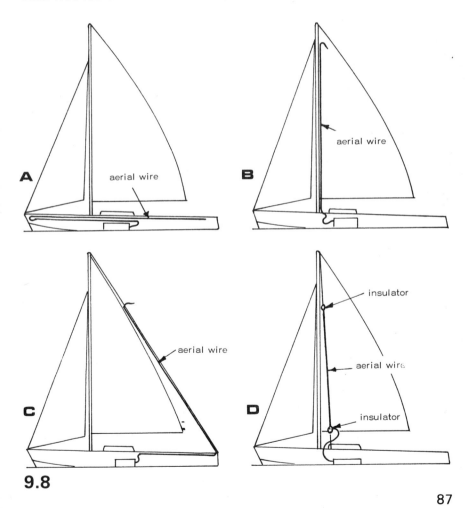

9.8

A possible alternative with metallic wire rigging is to use one of the shrouds as the aerial, i.e. like position D but with the receiver aerial wire cut short and connecting to a further length of shroud to give the same total aerial length. In this case the 'aerial' length incorporated in the shroud, *must* be separated from the other two portions of the shroud by insulators capable of taking the tension loading on the shroud. The weakness of this system is that the receiver aerial wire needs to have a demountable connection to the shroud—e.g. a small plug and socket—which may be subject to corrosion and poor contact after a period of use.

CHAPTER 10

SAIL WINCHES AND S.C.U. s

For adjusting the setting of sails by radio control a special type of servo is required both to accommodate the fairly long sheet movements that may be required, and to provide adequate power when pulling against wind pressure on sails (which may be of the order of ten pounds or more on larger yachts). Choice lies between a *sail winch* and a *sail control unit* (commonly referred to as a S.C.U.).

A *sail winch* is basically a servo with a high reduction gear ratio and fitted with a drum, or two drums, on the output spindle. Unlike a conventional servo, 'full' movement gives several revolutions of the drum, enabling a substantial length of sheet (line) to be winched in, or winched out. The Futaba sail winch, for example, provides a sheet travel of approximately 21 inches at a sheet hauling speed of $3\frac{1}{2}$ inches per second.

High reduction gearing ensures force-multiplication from a conventional size of servo motor, but sail winch servos are often larger than conventional types, with more powerful motors to produce even greater pulls. The Futaba sail winch generates a maximum pull of 15 pounds. Since the larger servo motor would overload a normal receiver battery, such sail winch servos are often designed to be worked off a separate 4.5 or 6 volt battery.

Apart from mechanical requirements—maximum pull, maximum sheet travel (an optimum working range to use is about 80 per cent of full travel), and sheet hauling speed—there is another important factor to be considered in choosing a commercial servo, but some will only work with a particular make of receiver. Thus the Graupner sail winch

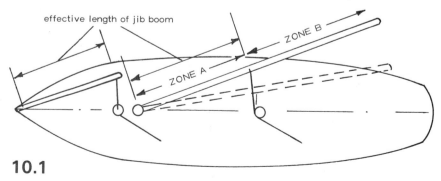

effective length of jib boom

ZONE A

ZONE B

10.1

10.2

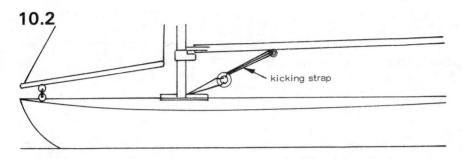

kicking strap

will only work with Graupner/Grundig radio. Many of the others—but not all—will work with most digital proportional receivers. In this case, however, they may need fitting with a matching plug to connect to a particular receiver.

Sail Setting 'Geometry'

As a general rule a change in sail setting requires the *same* movement of jib boom and main boom. Any differential—e.g. jib sheet setting slightly more close hauled than the mainsail—can be set up by initial manual adjustment with bowsies (see Chapter 9). A single drum winch will give this type of sail setting movement of the attachment point if the main sheet to the main boom is at a point equal to the effective length of the jib boom—Fig. 10.1.

Any other attachment point for the main sheet will give differential movement. Attaching the main sheet nearer the gooseneck will give progressively greater main boom movement than jib travel (zone A). Attaching the main sheet farther aft along the boom—zone B—will give progressively smaller main boom movement than jib travel. Here it should be borne in mind that attachment of the main sheet in zone A will require more servo pull for the same sail setting effort (i.e. against wind pressure) than if the attachment point is in zone B.

10.3

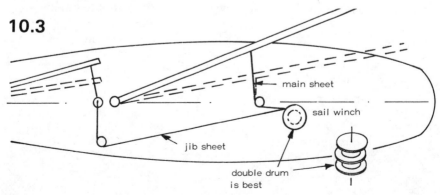

main sheet

sail winch

jib sheet

double drum
is best

As a general guide, a pull of at least 10 pounds is desirable from a sail winch (except for smaller yachts under 36 in. long which are unlikely to need more than about 6 pounds). Sheet hauling speed is not usually a critical factor. Again as a general guide a full movement or transit time of 5 to 6 seconds will be more than adequate, and up to 10 seconds should be acceptable.

Another practical point is that for effective sail setting the booms should not ride up or lift as this will result in 'spilling' wind from the sails. The main boom should be held down by a *kicking strap,* either of rubber or strong line—Fig. 10.1. The jib boom is more easily controlled simply by setting its forward pivot point a little way back along the boom. The pivot itself can be formed by a hook-and-eye system on smaller yachts. On larger yachts it is usually a fishing line swivel.

Whatever the attachment point adopted, the 'feed' point for the main sheet should be such that the sheet is substantially at 90 degrees to the boom in its close-hauled position, i.e. pulling at *right angles* to the boom in this position. If the sheet pulls at a substantially acute angle to the boom it will require excessive hauling power and put high stresses on the 'feed' pulley or fairlead to achieve a close-hauled setting. Similar considerations apply with the jib sheet, although here locating the jib sheet fairlead in line with the end of the boom is satisfactory.

In planning the sheet layout the length of sheet travel required should also be considered. This has to be enough to give a boom movement of up to 70 degrees—i.e. from 10 degrees close hauled to 80 degrees for 'running' setting (see also Chapter 9). As a rough guide, this will require a sheet travel at least equal to the distance from the gooseneck to the attachment point of the main sheet on the main boom.

Using Sail Winches

The simplest method of rigging a sail winch is to take both sheets directly to the winch drum, as shown in Fig. 10.3. Sheet travel available is then equal to the full 'travel' of the winch, as determined by the drum diameter and number of revolutions available from the winch movement (sheet travel=3.14 *times* drum diameter). A divided or *double drum* is best so that the main and jib sheets are wound on separate sections of the drum. In this case the sheet attached to the top part of the drum should go through a separate 'feed' so that it runs directly to the drum without rubbing on the central flange.

The use of a double drum with different diameters (a differential drum) gives different hauling speeds for jib and main sheets. This can be used to obtain differential settings, if required. More usually it is employed to enable the main sheet to be attached further aft along the main boom, with the main sheet attached to the larger drum diameter—Fig. 10.4.

10.4

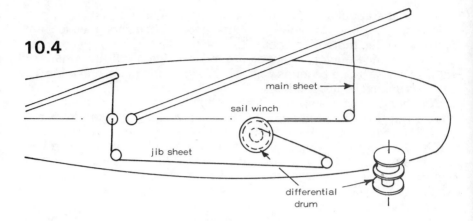

main sheet

sail winch

jib sheet

differential drum

The main limitation of both these simple systems is that they rely on wind pressure on the sails to keep the sheets taut. When there is no sail pressure the sheets will tend to go slack and can easily unwind a turn or two off the drum, or snag up on each other and tangle on the drum. To avoid this a single line only can be wound on the winch drum, connecting to separate main and jib sheets—Fig. 10.5. A length of small section rubber strip, with tension adjusted by a bowsie, is then connected to this joint point to ensure that the line around the drum itself is always in tension. To avoid excessive maximum tension (which is acting against the pull of the winch) a fairly long run of rubber is desirable.

In planning the layout of such a system it is important to allow for adequate travel. This must be realised without the join point actually reaching the drum.

A further system is shown in Fig. 10.6, again using a double drum of the same diameter. The winch line runs from the top drum, around a pulley and back to the bottom drum. Thus no further tensioning is

10.5

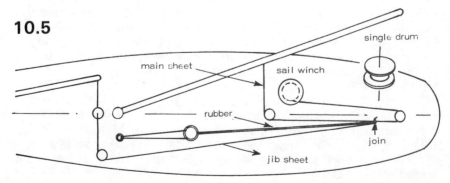

single drum

main sheet

sail winch

rubber

join

jib sheet

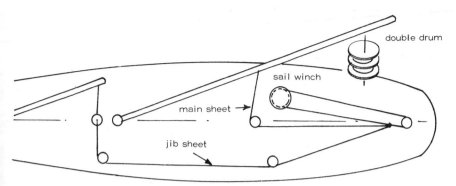

double drum

sail winch

main sheet →

jib sheet

10.6

needed to maintain the drum line taut. Jib and main sheets attach to a common point on one side of this run.

With this system, pulley position is important. The distance between drum and pulley needs to be at least equal to the sheet haul movement required in order to avoid any possibility of winding the sheet join point either around the bottom half of the drum, or around the pulley itself. It is necessary to consider the *maximum* winch travel available as although this may not normally be required, it could be produced accidentally (e.g. by a prolonged transmitter signal).

Sail Control Units

Sail control units range from home-made winches to lever systems and also include a number of proprietary designs. They fall into two main categories: (i) adaptations of conventional servos; and (ii) separate mechanisms which are controlled by a switch or switches operated by a conventional servo. To this could be added a very limited number of proprietary items which are complete in themselves and thus classified as special servos.

Lever systems will appeal particularly to mechanically minded modellers as they can be designed to be operated by conventional servos. Theoretically it is only a matter of 'multiplying' the normal push-pull movement of a conventional servo to get the required amount of sheet hauling travel. In practice the degree of multiplication of movement can prove impractical, unless limited to fairly restricted sheet travels.

Two basic lever movements operated directly by a conventional servo are shown in Fig. 10.7, using a linear servo. Since the full push-pull travel of a linear servo is only of the order of $\frac{5}{8}$ inch a very long lever is needed to get appreciable sheet travel movement. A horizontal lever is usually best since there is normally more space available across the beam of a hull than in the depth, so a longer lever can be used. It can also be installed fully below the deck, taking the sheets out through

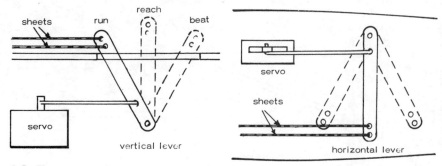

sheets   run   reach   beat

servo

vertical lever

servo

sheets

horizontal lever

10.7

fairleads. In both cases the servo output force decreases in proportion to the movement multiplication. Thus if the lever multiplies the movement by say, 10 (still only giving a travel of about 6 inches), the force available for sheet hauling is only 1/10th of the servo output force as applied to the lever. This reduction in force available from a conventional servo virtually makes it largely impractical to provide further multiplication of sheet travel via pulley blocks, which could otherwise be an answer to limited lever movement.

Actually this overstates the limitations of lever movements, particularly for racing yachts. Only limited sheet haul movements are necessary for sailing a particular course. Thus after completing a beat, for example, sails would be retrimmed manually in preparation for the following run. In other words, with initial manual sail setting to nominal position, lever movements should then be more than capable of providing adequate sheet haul travel for any adjustments necessary in sailing a beat *or* run *or* reach, as required.

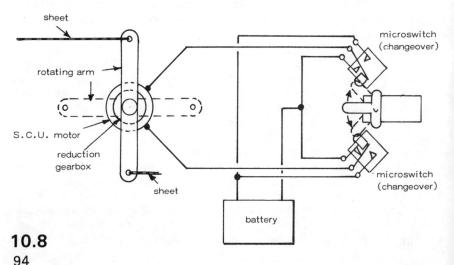

sheet

rotating arm

S.C.U. motor

reduction gearbox

sheet

microswitch (changeover)

microswitch (changeover)

battery

10.8

94

S.C.U. output movement

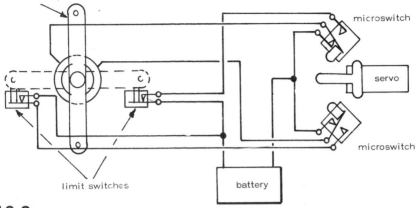

limit switches

battery

10.9

An alternative application of lever movement for sheet hauling is to drive the lever by a separate electric motor through reduction gearing. Lever movement can then be up to 180 degrees if required and, because reduction gearing will *multiply* rather than divide the torque output of the motor, any further adjustment of movement required can be provided by passing the sheet(s) through pulley blocks. Unfortunately since most small DC motors run at quite high speeds a very large reduction ratio is needed—usually something of the order of 2,000 to 1. Even Pile gearboxes only give reduction ratios up to 360:1 which may still not be enough. Multiple worm gearing may be necessary, with the penalty of higher torque losses.

Nevertheless, a motor-driven lever system can prove very successful, properly designed and installed. The other complication is working it from the radio control system.

The do-it-yourself method for this is to use a conventional servo as the master control, operating a microswitch at each limit position of its travel—i.e. the switches are so mounted on or adjacent to the servo so that the output arm operates the switch movement when the servo drives to its limit position(s). These switches are then wired to the electric motor and a separate battery as shown in Fig. 10.8.

One other refinement is necessary in this circuit. Two more switches must be incorporated, operated by the S.C.U. lever at the ends of *its* travel. These 'break' the motor circuit when the lever reaches its limit position and prevent the motor continuing to rotate the lever—Fig. 10.9.

To operate the S.C.U. in one direction, the transmitter stick is moved to one full movement position and held there for as long as necessary for the lever to move to the position required. The signal is then released, causing the servo to self-centre, breaking the motor circuit.

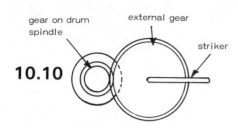

gear on drum spindle

external gear

striker

10.10

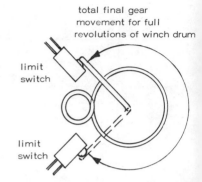

total final gear movement for full revolutions of winch drum

limit switch

limit switch

To operate in the other direction, the same action is taken with the transmitter stick moved to its other full movement position. In this way the final position of the lever can be 'inched' one way or the other, as required.

The limit switches operated by the lever only come into operation if the transmitter signal is held on so long that the lever comes to the end of its practical movement. They simply prevent the lever over-running. Thus sail setting is a *progressive* control which of course is inferior to proportional control since the setting required has to be established on a 'trial and error' basis.

The same principle of construction can also be used for a sail winch, i.e. fitting a drum on the output spindle of the gearbox rather than a lever. In this case a reduction ratio of 150:1 to 250:1 should prove satisfactory. Another reason for preferring a drum for winching rather than a lever is that sheet travel is not restricted by mechanical movements. The drum can be allowed to rotate as many times as necessary to achieve the required travel. In other words, it operates just like a conventional sail winch, except that it again has to be controlled by switching through a separate circuit with the switches operated by a conventional servo as in Fig. 10.8. Thus it has the same

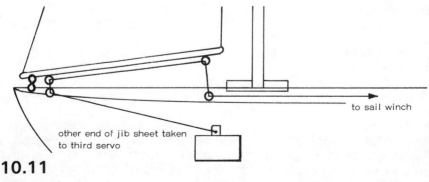

to sail winch

other end of jib sheet taken to third servo

10.11

limitation as the motorised lever. It is a *progressive* type of control, not a proportional control as provided by a conventional sail winch.

There is one other difficulty, too, with this type of sail winch. Whereas with a lever movement it is easy to position limit switches to break the motor circuit and stop the lever at the ends of its travel, this is not readily possible when the output movement is a rotating drum. Thus if for any reason the signal is held on too long the winch will unwind or wind in to the limit of the line length available and then stall with the motor still trying to drive. This can either break the line (unlikely) or stall the servo operating the motor on-off switching.

On this basis, many modellers prefer a lever system to a motorised winch for a S.C.U. However, it is possible to arrange for limit switching with a drum output by driving an external gear (or gear train) from the drum spindle giving a reduction ratio numerically equal to a little less than twice the number of full revolutions the winch drum can perform. This means that for full revolution of the drum the external gear (or final gear) will turn through less than a full revolution—not more than about 270 degrees.

This final gear is fitted with a striker arm, and microswitches are positioned at each end of the movement to work as limit switches. Thus when the drum rotates to its limit of revolutions one way the striker will operate the limit switch and switch the drum motor off. Similarly, as the drum approaches its limit of revolutions in the opposite direction, the second limit switch will operate to switch it off again—Fig. 10.10. Wiring for this system is exactly the same as in Fig. 10.9.

Fine Trimming with a Third Servo

Whilst a proportional sail winch (or a S.C.U. which works *proportionally* rather than progressively) can provide quite accurate sail setting with suitable rigging, it still lacks the final touch for fine trimming. This really requires provision to be able to adjust the jib independently, after setting the main sail to its optimum position. This can be an important feature in racing and the only really satisfactory method of achieving it is via a third, proportional servo (calling for 3-channel radio).

Assuming that jib and mainsail are operated by a conventional winch, the only difference is that the jib sheet is not made off on the jib boom but runs down to this third servo—Fig. 10.11. Maximum travel required is not likely to be more than 2 or 3 inches from the third servo, but this is still in excess of the movement provided by a standard output arm. Thus whilst a conventional (proportional) servo is quite satisfactory for the purpose, it will usually have to be fitted with a longer output arm. Another point to consider is that with a larger yacht the power of a standard 'aircraft' servo may not be adequate. If this is suspected, then a more powerful *proportional* servo should be used.

'Jib-Twitching'

An alternative use for a third servo is 'jib twitching' or pulling the jib to the opposite side to the mainsail for 'goosewinging' when the sails have been set for a run. This may even be worthwhile considering as an additional control to jib trimming; but in this case a separate servo should be used for each, i.e. demanding a total of four servos in all (and 4-channel radio). Although 'jib twitching' is only required on a run where jib trimming is not very necessary, and jib trimming is advantageous on all other courses, it is difficult to adapt *one* servo to do both jobs.

Given the choice between the two (i.e. restricting control coverage to 3-channel radio), jib trimming would be preferred choice for the third control. It is usually possible to produce 'goosewinging' by manipulation of the helm if this does not happen naturally when a yacht is on a true run.

Traveller-type Sheet Haul

The traveller-type sheet haul is probably simpler to make than a lever or winch S.C.U., since it does not require the same high reduction gearing. It consists of a threaded rod forming a spindle and driven through reduction gearing by an electric motor. On this rod is a traveller, consisting of a nut attached to an extension piece or traveller arm. To prevent the nut rotating a rigid wire is mounted parallel to the rod, passing through a hole in the arm. (Alternatively, the fact that the arm traverses along a slot in the deck will prevent it from rotating, but in this case both sides of the slot need facing with a suitable bearing surface—preferably a strip of PTFE plastic to minimise friction). Thus when the threaded rod spindle is rotated by the motor the traveller arm is driven along the length of the rod (and in the reverse direction if the motor is reversed). Sheets are attached to the end of the traveller arm for sail setting—Fig. 10.12.

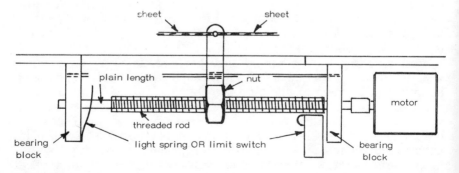

10.12

This type of S.C.U. is switch controlled by a conventional servo in the same manner as Fig. 10.9. Limit switches can also be fitted near each end of the rod, actuated when the traveller reaches its end position. Alternatively the necessity for limit switches can be avoided by turning the ends of the threaded rod down to a plain section. Thus when the traveller (nut) comes to the other end of the rod it runs onto the plain section. At this point it is no longer driven. To ensure that the nut picks up the thread when the motor is reversed, light springs are necessary at each end of the rod.

A traveller system is best designed to fit under the deck, otherwise it requires a long slot in the deck to accommodate traveller movement which simply asks for water to get into the hull (and on the traveller mechanism).

One advantage of a traveller system is that it is easy to design for a given sheet haul length and hauling speed. Sheet haul movement is simply the length of the threaded rod, which can be selected accordingly. Hauling speed then depends on the reduction gearing between motor and threaded rod, and the number of threads per inch on the rod. The latter is equivalent to 'worm gearing' and the reduction ratio achieved may be high enough to eliminate the need for any reduction gearing between motor and threaded rod.

For example, taking 6,000 rpm as the estimated running speed under load of the motor to be used and using a 4BA threaded rod, the number of threads per inch on the rod is 38.45—say 40. Driven *directly* by the motor this would give a traveller speed of 6,000÷40=150 inches per minute=2.5 inches per second.

CHAPTER 11

ELECTRIC MOTOR SUPPRESSION

When running, electric motors generate wide-band electrical 'signals' which can interfere with the performance of a receiver unless the motor is suppressed. (An unsuppressed motor running near a domestic radio, for example, will generally produce a 'crackle' over the whole tuning range of the set). Fortunately suppression is quite easy, and many motors produced as marine propulsion units do already incorporate suppression. (If in doubt, try running it near a domestic radio or television set).

The simplest method of suppression is to connect a *capacitor* across the motor—Fig. 11.1A. The capacitor value is not critical—usually anything between .01 and .05 microfarads will prove satisfactory. To be made effective it should be connected directly across the *brushes* of the motor using *soldered* connections; but connecting directly across the motor terminals may be easier, and nearly as good.

A better system, recommended for larger or more powerful motors, is to use two capacitors. Each is connected between a brush (or motor terminal) and the *metal* casing of the motor—Fig. 11.1B. The motor itself should also be 'earthed'.

If the motor, when installed, is connected to the propeller shaft via a metal coupling, it will automatically be 'earthed' when the boat is in the water. If the coupling is plastic, however, or incorporates non metallic parts separating motor spindle from the propeller shaft, a separate earthing wire should be taken from the motor casing to the stern tube. This is another example of bonding (see also Chapter 14).

11.1

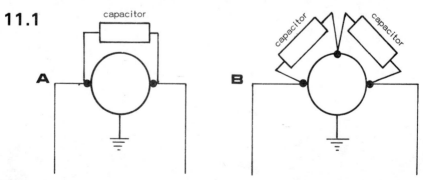

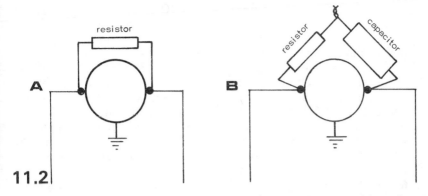

11.2

If a capacitor (or pair of capacitors) does not provide adequate suppression, other methods can be tried. The simplest alternative is to use a *resistor* connected directly across the motor—Fig. 11.2A. This should be of five to ten times the nominal resistance of the electric motor to avoid 'starving' the motor of current. For small to medium size motors a value of 47 or 100 ohms should be about right. This suppression circuit can be 'broken' as far as direct current is concerned by connecting a capacitor (.01 to .1 microfarads in series with the resistor—Fig. 11.2B. This should make suppression even more effective and not drain any current away from the motor.

There are more elaborate methods of suppression which can be used if necessary. For smaller motors two diodes connected back-to-back across the motor can be tried—Fig. 11.3A. For larger motors which appear to be particularly 'dirty' as regards generation of interference, the system shown in Fig. 11.3B should provide a suitable answer. This provides capacitor suppression across the motor together with a radio frequency choke (RFC) in each motor lead. A suitable valve

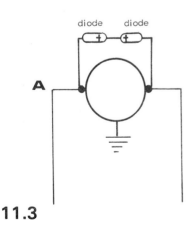

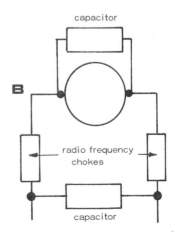

11.3

for these chokes would be 70-100 microhenrys. A second capacitor can also be added across the battery side of the chokes.

In all cases components used for suppression—capacitors, resistors or diodes, should be of adequate *rating* for the job—i.e. be rated for use at the motor battery voltage and maximum wattage that the circuit is likely to handle. *Watts* equals volts×amps. Thus, with a 6 volt motor, for example, where the maximum current drain could be, say, 1 amp, the maximum *rating* for the circuit would be 6×1=6 watts.

Components used in bypass (parallel) circuits will only be subject to a fraction of this maximum wattage, but in the case of resistors and diodes remember that component ratings can start as low as 1/20 watt.

Components used in bypass (parallel) circuits will only be subject to sion motors for electric-powered boats and electric motors used to power home-made sail control units and ancillary services. Some propulsion motors produced primarily as marine power units may already incorporate adequate suppression, but all 'plain' electric motors needs suppression. Even switching contacts can cause interference by arcing on 'break'. Here a capacitor connected across the switch contacts will provide suppression if necessary without interfering with the DC working of the switch.

Servos, and other proprietary radio control units, do not need additional suppression. This has been taken care of in their design.

CHAPTER 12

OPERATIONAL TECHNIQUES

All modern radio gear is switch-on-and-go. There are no adjustments to make (other than adjustments to the control linkages to arrive at the required control movements). This is not quite as foolproof as it may appear for one of the things that is surprisingly often forgotten is to switch on the receiver before setting a boat under way! So pre-launch checks should be the order of the day.

(i) First make sure that the Tx and Rx batteries are fully charged *before* leaving for the pond.

(ii) Switch on Tx and Rx and check for correct operation of all control, again *before* leaving for the pond.

(iii) If the model is a powerboat fitted with a whip aerial—make sure that the aerial *is* in place.

(iv) Check all operation of controls before starting the engine (or switching on the propulsion motor) with the boat in the water at the pond side.

(v) Check out operation of the controls again with the engine running *before* releasing the boat. (In the case of an I/C engined boat you would normally switch the radio off after (iv)). This is an essential final check. Remember the basic switch-on, switch-off rules:

Switch on

Generally recommended practice is to switch on the *Transmitter* first, then the Receiver. Remember that servos will only assume their 'working' neutral position when both the Tx and Rx are switched on.

Switch off

The reverse applies when switching off. Switch the *Receiver* off first, then the Transmitter.

Make sure that you know which is the 'on' and 'off' position of the receiver switch. The switch supplied with the receiver is not always marked 'on' and 'off' (although on some the exposed slide part when 'on' may be coloured red). If you have installed your radio on a watertight box the switch should be operated by an extension wire (see Chapter 4). Pushing this wire *down* should switch 'on' with yachts.

Using the Control Sticks

Nobody can really tell you how to manipulate the control sticks properly. This will only come with practice. Beginners usually over-control, i.e. use too much stick movement, and also tend to over-correct with jerky movements. Remember that controls respond *proportionately,* so smooth stick movements will produce smooth control movements. Fortunately over-control and over-correction—the tendency beginners have to resist—is seldom critical or dangerous, although it can produce somewhat dramatic results with a fast powerboat.

The more clear space you have to operate in the better, for a start, so choose a quiet time for your first attempts, or trying out a new boat. If over-control on rudder persists as a problem, then reducing rudder movement may help (re-position the pushrod in a hole farther away from the rudder shaft on the tiller arm). Also check out the response to rudder *trim* movement instead of stick movement. If this produces strong responses, the rudder *area* could be too large.

Think 'Aboard'!

Steering a boat by radio is easy—as long as the craft is moving away from you! It is far from easy at first when the boat has made a 180 degree turn and is heading back towards you because the rudder control 'sense' is now reversed. An instinctive stick (or wheel) movement to port on the transmitter will make the model turn to starboard, and vice versa.

The answer is always to think and react *as if you were aboard the craft*—not as a 'spectator' on the land. It is a knack which is only gained with practice. Until this knack is acquired, some beginners find it easiest to shut their eyes momentarily to work out which way they should move the rudder control. Not a practice to be recommended when controlling a high speed boat—but it does appear to work with some people! Others have found it helpful to turn the transmitter the wrong way round and operate the rudder stick by reaching over the top of the transmitter case. It should not take long, however, for the absolute beginner to acquire this knack of mentally 'travelling aboard' the craft, 'looking' towards the bow.

Range

Modern radio control systems used with aircraft have a ground-to-air range of several miles—virtually out-of-sight range. The same equipment used in boats has substantially reduced range, perhaps less than a mile under even the most favourable conditions. However, for all R/C boat operation the range provided by standard equipment is usually more than adequate, unless adversely affected by individual circumstances. These include poor receiver aerial efficiency (e.g. receiver aerial too short), the presence of large buildings and, of course, interference—about which little can be done. Lack of range is *generally* the result of either weak batteries or poor receiver aerial positioning.

You can easily check the range of your radio equipment, but this should always be done under normal operating conditions. Moor the boat at one end of the pond in the water with the radio switched on. Leave a helper with it, with instructions to give an arm signal when the rudder control works (he can listen for the servo moving). Walk right down to the other end—and beyond as long as you can still see your assistant. Operate the transmitter (rudder control) and check that your assistant confirms that it works. (Remember to switch the transmitter on first!).

If you cannot proceed farther than the end of the pond of which you want to check that you have range in hand, *half close* the transmitter telescopic aerial before signalling. If your receiver responds to this weakened signal, you should have ample range in hand. *Do not* fully close the transmitter aerial, or remove it, for a check like this. Signalling with no aerial in place on the transmitter could damage the circuitry.

The way the transmitter is held also affects its range. The signal radiated from the Tx aerial is of maximum strength in a direction at

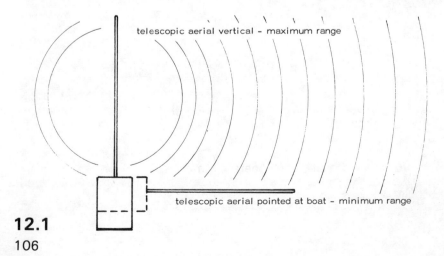

telescopic aerial vertical - maximum range

telescopic aerial pointed at boat - minimum range

12.1

right angles to the aerial and a minimum in line with the aerial—Fig. 12.1. Thus turning the transmitter to point the aerial *at* the boat will give *minimum* range (and even in some cases no signal at all at the receiver). Thus the transmitter should always be held so that the aerial is pointing upwards. Any upward angle of 45 degrees or more is quite adequate. If you think the boat is approaching extreme radio range, angle the Tx aerial upward even more to 90 degrees—*not* downwards to point at the boat.

Co-operation with other Modellers

When more than one modeller wants to operate a radio controlled model on the same site, each must operate on a different 'spot' frequency. This means selecting (or choosing) the Tx and Rx crystals to be used accordingly.

First choice would be to select a 'spot' frequency at least one standard 'spot' away to minimise any risk of interference. That will allow up to six modellers to operate simultaneously on the 27 MHz band. If more than six modellers wish to operate at the same time, then the split frequency spots should be utilised (see Appendix II).

Bearing in mind the previous comments under 'Range', again operating a model radio control transmitter within a mile of the site

107

may be 'commanding' a particular spot frequency; or at least causing interference on that 'spot'. This operator may not be in sight (he could be 'testing' in a house nearby, for example). This will show up using the switch-on, switch-off technique previously described.

Radio Troubles

Radio troubles due to component failure are comparatively rare, unless the equipment has been abused. They are not unknown, of course, but what is commonly blamed as 'faulty radio' is very much more likely to be something else.

These are the most likely causes of poor radio performance:—

    (i)   Weak batteries—by far the most common fault.

    (ii)   Poor connections—plug and socket connections into the receiver corroded, pins bent or damaged, or dirty.

    (iii)   Sticking or binding servo pushrod movements.

    (iv)   Receiver aerial too short, poorly positioned, or 'earthed' through moisture or contact with metal components.

    (v)   Interference causing erratic and unwanted servo response or 'glitching'. (Interference on the 27 MHz band can arise from other sources than another modeller's radio transmitter—e.g. Citizens Band radio).

Checking Your Radio For Faults

A suspected flat receiver battery can be checked by replacing with another freshly charged battery (or batteries in the case of a drycell outfit). Testing the battery voltage with a meter is not necessarily a positive check—see Chapter 13.

If a servo appears faulty, check by replacing temporarily with another servo. For example, if the rudder servo does not appear to be working properly, unplug it from the receiver and plug the throttle servo into its position. If the same fault is apparent, then the first servo is not faulty. If the fault is cleared, the original servo is faulty.

By 'replacing' a rudder servo in this way you may be able to continue operating at the expense of loss of one control service.

This idea of 'substitution' can also be used to check a receiver for correct operation. If you do not have a spare receiver you may be able to borrow one from someone else who has the same make of equipment. A substitution check takes only a few minutes to carry out and receivers are of course—or should be—readily removable from any boat installation. Make sure, however, that the substitute receiver you are using is filed with a crystal matching your transmitter.

Servos or receivers which are found to be faulty—or are not working due to mechnical damage or immersion—must be returned to a recognised service agent for the make of radio involved. They should be returned with a note of the circumstances under which the fault appeared. Attempted repairs by non-specialists can result in permanent damage—meaning that you may well end up by having to buy a new receiver and/or servos.

CHAPTER 13

BATTERIES

The standard size of battery usually supplied for the receiver with Nicad Tx-Rx Combos is usually 450 mAh (four cylindrical AA size Nicad cells), meaning that the battery has a capacity of 450 milliamp-hours—i.e. capable of accommodating a discharge rate of 450 milliamps for a period of one hour, or pro rata.

The receiver battery supplies both the receiver and the servos (except some special duty servos, like sail winches, which may work off a separate battery). Actual discharge rate will therefore vary with the number of servos being used, and the amount of time they are in use. A 450 mAh battery capacity is generally more than adequate for operating aircraft controls over a typical day's flying time. Boats may be operated for longer periods at a time, but normally with fewer servos. Only experience—i.e. how long you normally run the boat and how frequently you use the controls—will show whether or not a standard battery size is adequate for your requirements. It should certainly be adequate for any normal single operation session. For repeated operation throughout a day, a standard battery may not have enough capacity. In this case it will be cheaper to buy a spare battery of the same size to change over to, rather than a larger capacity Nicad battery.

Battery life is far shorter with a drycell Combo. Again only experience will indicate the likely life of a set of dry batteries. To be on the safe side you need to change batteries frequently. Although they cost about three times as much AA size, *alkaline-manganese batteries* are a much better proposition than HP7 cells. They will last as much as *ten* times longer. In fact, in AA size their *capacity* is greater than the same size of Nicads, but they are not rechargeable like Nicads.

Since Nicad cells are available in the same physical size as HP7 batteries (AA size), it would seem a simple matter to convert an all-drycell Combo to Nicads simply by buying a set of Nicad cells to fit the same battery box. The cost of doing this would be about 10 to 12 times that of a set of ordinary drycells (HP7s), but cheaper than buying a made-up Nicad battery *pack* for conversion.

Unfortunately this may not work. The receiver of a drycell Combo normally works on 6 volts (four HP7 dry batteries). Four *Nicad* cells of similar size will only give 4.8 volts (Nicad cells give 1.2 volts per cell as against 1.5 volts per cell with dry batteries). This may not be sufficient

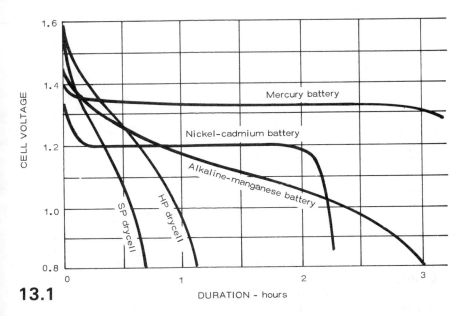

13.1 DURATION - hours

voltage to operate a receiver *designed* for drycell operation. It would need an extra Nicad cell to bring up to voltage—and this would not fit in the battery box.

This may not be the case with *all* drycell receivers. Nicad receivers are normally designed to work on 4.8 volts (with a battery pack containing four Nicad cells). Some drycell receivers *are* designed with conversion in mind—i.e. are designed to work on 6 volts (drycells) down to 4.8 volts (Nicads). In this case replacing drycells in a standard battery box with equivalent size Nicad cells would work.

Similar comments apply to drycell transmitter batteries (typically eight AA size (HP7) drycells, giving 12 volts. AA size alkaline-manganese batteries will give a much more reliable performance than ordinary dry batteries (HP7s). And similar 'conversion' problems *may* arise if you try to change to a Nicad battery.

One other point about alkaline-manganese cells. They are easy to confuse with *mercury* cells which are almost identical in appearance in AA size. Mercury cells are even more expensive, but have even better capacity, than an equivalent alkaline-manganese cell. They generate only 1.4 volts per cell—but this difference in voltage would not normally affect the working of a drycell receiver.

Fig. 13.1 shows typical performance characteristics of AA size batteries of different types, all subject to a current drain of the order of 200-250 milliamps. (This is about the average current drain of a 3- or 4-channel transmitter; and also that of the current drain on a receiver battery when working two servos). Even an HP type drycell drops its

111

voltage rapidly with *continuous* load—but it 'recovers' if allowed to rest—and its ultimate capacity is far less than the other types of the same physical size.

The suitability of an alternative battery type for a drycell transmitter or receiver, however, basically depends on the acceptable 'end voltage' the circuits will accommodate. If this is 1.3 volts, for example, then the same number of Nicad cells would not be satisfactory and even an alakaline-manganese battery might not have as long a 'life' as an HP drycell.

By far the most common cause of radio failure is a flat receiver battery or transmitter battery. So the state of the batteries is one of the most vital aspects of successful radio control operation.

Checking the State of the Battery

Transmitters are commonly fitted with a *battery condition indicator,* which is merely a voltmeter showing the battery voltage when the transmitter is switched on. It will give a reasonable indication of the state of dry batteries in a drycell Tx, as the indicated voltage will fall progressively as the Tx battery becomes more and more discharged. It will not give the same indication with a *Nicad* Tx battery as this will maintain the *same* output voltage until the battery is almost discharged. Then voltage will drop suddenly.

For the same reason it is not possible to check the state of a Nicad receiver battery by simple measurement of voltage across the battery. It will show a 'full' voltage until it is almost discharged. But a more meaningful reading can be made with a voltmeter and a receiver dry battery, provided the measure is made with the receiver switched on and under load (e.g. by operating one servo). Fig. 13.1 showing typical voltage/discharge characteristics for AA size dry battery cells can be useful in estimating the likely condition of an Rx dry battery pack from measured voltage under load.

Recharging Nicad Batteries

Ideally Nicad batteries should be fully charged the day before a session of use. This is a simple enough operation since most Nicad Combos are supplied with a matching charger which plugs into a normal 240 main voltage supply, with separate output loads for charging the Tx and Rx batteries simultaneously. The trouble is deciding how much (how long) a charge is necessary as the initial state of the battery is really unknown.

Probably for normal operation this is not really a problem. The charger, as supplied with the set, will normally be designed to charge at the 1/10th rate, i.e. provide a full charge in a flat battery in 15 hours.

112

It is not harmful to overcharge Nicad batteries at this 1/10th rate, so even if the battery is only partially discharged, giving it a 'full' charge time at this rate is quite acceptable practice and consistent with the time provided by a full 'overnight' charge.

The one thing that can go wrong is simple human forgetfulness—leaving the batteries on for an excessive charging time (perhaps the whole of the next day), for example. Or even forgetting that the charge is plugged into a mains point and accidentally switching off that point when switching off the lights on leaving the room for the night.

Different considerations apply if a shorter charging time is required—e.g. charging at a higher rate and reducing the charging time accordingly. Sealed Nicad cells can be charged at about twice the 1/10th rate without coming to harm, provided they are not *overcharged*. Charging at even higher rates, with correspondingly shortened charging time is only possible with *vented* Nicad cells *designed* to accommodate high charging rates.

This can be a little confusing. *Button type* Nicad cells are *sealed* and should *never* be rapid-charged, or drastically overcharged even at low rate. If they are, at least they will overheat, distort and be ruined. If *rapid-charged,* they will probably explode.

Cylindrical (e.g. AA size) Nicad cells *are* vented. These are the type now most widely supplied with all-Nicad Combos. They will accept over-charging with less risk of damage, but excessively overcharged they will still overheat and become damaged. They are not *necessarily* suitable for *rapid-charging,* however. But they can be charged at higher than the normal 1/10th rate if necessary in emergencies.

The only satisfactory method of control with higher charge rates is first to discharge the Nicad battery under controlled conditions, and then give it the *correct* time for a full charge. Correct time can be calculated as:—1.5 x charging rate x time (hours) *equals* specified battery capacity.

Chargers usually work at a predetermined charging rate (or have provision for adjusting the charging rate) when:

$$\text{charging time (hrs)} = \frac{\text{stated battery capacity mAh}}{1.5 \times \text{charging rate (mA)}}$$

The most suitable unit for this is a Nicad *charger/discharger.* After connection, the Nicad battery can first be fully discharged by the unit, then switched to charge for the required time.

It is also good practice to use a charger/discharger to discharge and fully charge both the Tx and Rx Nicad batteries at regular periods in order to ensure that simple 'overnight' charging using the Combo charger has not got out of step with actual battery requirements.

Another type of problem arrives if the Rx battery size has been charged from the standard one supplied. The charger supplied with the

Combo will no longer fully charge the larger Rx battery in the same time as it does the (original) Tx battery.

If the Rx battery has been charged to one having to *double* the capacity it really needs charging by a separate charger at *twice* the charge rate the Combo charger can provide, otherwise it will only be charging at *half* the 1/10th rate. This will need more than twice the original charging time—well over 30 hours to recharge a fully discharged Rx battery.

If using a separate charger for Nicads, remember the simple, safe rules:

(i) Charging current required (milliamp) $= \dfrac{\text{stated battery capacity (mAh)}}{10}$

(ii) Safe minimum charging time=10 hours*.

(iii) Nominal maximum charging time=15 hours†

(iv) Charging time not to be exceeded=20 hours.

*This will ensure virtually full charge on any battery which is not fully discharged.

†This will ensure a full charge irrespective of the initial state of the battery.

CHAPTER 14

CORROSION—AND EMERGENCY ACTIONS!

Model boats spend only relative short periods actually in contact with water, so corrosion is not the same problem as it is with full size craft. However, almost everything concerned with electrics—which means every part of a radio control system—is particularly susceptible to the effects of dampness and corrosion. These may need special care or treatment, if harmful results are to be avoided.

All corrosion is electrolytic in nature (even simple rusting of iron and steel) and is the product of 'active' galvanic cells being set up—e.g. by two dissimilar metals in contact, or even local metallurgical differences in a single piece of metal. To become active these cells require the presence of an electrolyte. Then they start to work like an elementary battery generating minute currents and with the positive element of the cell (or anode) being gradually eaten away.

Fresh water is a very weak electrode, so boats operated in fresh water ponds or lakes should not experience many corrosion problems, other than rusting of any steel parts. Contact materials or radio control plugs and sockets and switches are normally safe in this respect, also wiring (which is protected by its insulation anyway). Salt water is a different matter entirely for this is a powerful electrolyte accelerating galvanic action and promoting rapid corrosion of many metals and metal combinations. Thus electrical components must be protected against contact with salt water or salt spray.

Here it is very important to remember that although salt water will dry off it will leave a deposit of salt behind it. Subsequently, if a model is kept in a damp atmosphere these salt deposits will absorb moisture from the atmosphere and turn into active electrolyte. Models which have been operated in salt water, therefore, should be washed down with fresh water and dried before being put away—and similar treatment given to flushing out and draining bilges if salt water has got inside the hull.

Ideally all the radio gear should be enclosed in watertight compartments (see Chapter 4), so water should not get in. Pushrods and switches are difficult, or impossible, to protect in this way, and so on a salt-water boat may need particular attention. Steel pushrods are generally to be avoided, as these will readily rust. Brass is a more suitable material for boats; or 'snakes' where a Bowden cable pushrod is fully enclosed in a plastic tube. In the latter case the exposed ends of

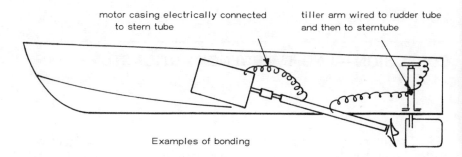

motor casing electrically connected to stern tube

tiller arm wired to rudder tube and then to sterntube

Examples of bonding

14.1

the cable can be protected with a regular light spray of water repellant/lubricant, such as WD40 or similar.

A regular light spray with WD40 is also recommended for exposed switches. If a switch has been splashed with salt water, first spray with fresh water to flush out any salt, then spray with WD40 which will effectively remove any remaining water and leave the surfaces lightly lubricated.

WD40 (or similar) water-repellant lubricant, should *not* be used on electric motors or *electronic circuits* (e.g. printed circuit boards) as they can produce a deposit build-up which can be harmful.

Where, through some accident (or lack of protection in installation), radio receivers or servos have become immersed in water, effectiveness of treatment depends very much on how soon remedial action can be taken. The sooner the better is the general rule.

Cases of radio *receivers* are not waterproof—so immersion or liberal splashing with water may well mean that water has got inside. If it is *fresh* water, opening the case, shaking out water and leaving to dry out in a warm (not too hot) atmosphere may be all that is necessary. If it is *salt* water, *wash* the whole receiver board with *fresh* water under a running tap, shake and dry with a hair dryer. This will not do any more harm than the salt water already has, and may save the day if the salt-water immersion has not been too long.

Many *servos* specified for marine use are quoted as 'waterproof'. Few are fully waterproof. Most are more correctly described as water-resistant, relying on O-ring or similar seals to keep water out during short periods of immersion. To check, following immersion, open the case and look for water inside. Then treat as for receivers except that if fresh water flushing is needed, try to direct this away from the *electric motor*. If water gets in the motor, it will probably stay there. Finally, after drying, spray the electric motor and potentiometer(s) with an *electrical contact cleaning fluid* in an aerosol can using the thin extension tube supplied with the can to direct the spray just where it is needed.

If after dunking in *fresh* water, and subsequent treatment as above, the receiver and servo(s) work normally, all is probably well. If they work after treatment for *salt* water immersion, they are still suspect—but if still O.K. after a week or so, again all is probably well. If performance is impaired, or they do not work at all, the only action is to return them for servicing, stating the circumstances which caused the trouble—e.g. so many hours immersion in fresh/salt water—*and any subsequent action you have taken.*

Plugs and Sockets

Contact pins and sockets or plug-and-socket connections on radio control components are commonly gold plated and so ostensibly immune from corrosion. This is not necessarily the case when they have been wetted with salt water or salt spray. The gold coating is so thin it is usually porous. Shake, wash with fresh water applied with a small paintbrush. Blow dry, then spray with WD40 or similar water repellant fluid.

Contacts on switches, etc may also be plated for minimum contact resistance and corrosion prevention. Most platings are effective against fresh water, but cadmium plating is best in salt water atmospheres. So if there is a choice with switches, relays, etc, choose those which have cadmium plated contacts for marine use.

Batteries

The majority of batteries used with most radio control systems are of nickel cadmium type enclosed within a stainless steel case. Casing corrosion is extremely unlikely, but corrosion can occur at connection points, or on connecting wires. Lead-acid accumulators are much more prone to corrosion developing on terminals. Such corrosion will start at a *positive* connection point (i.e. where connected to the positive side of a battery cell), and can spread from there. It can be eliminated by smearing the positive (or preferably both) battery terminal(s) with a special battery grease (obtainable from most garages). Note that with plug-in battery connections, the part where corrosion may start is the positive pin/socket connection.

Battery (terminal) corrosion is unlikely to occur at all if batteries are removed from the model when not in use for any appreciable time, e.g. 1-month for a model operated in fresh water and 1-week for a model operated in salt water.

Galvanic Currents

Electrical currents generated by galvanic (corrosion) cells are quite small and are unlikely to cause any radio interference under the most adverse conditions—e.g. two metals widely separated on the galvanic scale being activated by contact with salt water. (A bad example here would be a stainless steel propeller shaft running in metallic contact with an aluminium tube, giving a cell voltage which could be as high as 0.9 volts).

Any possibility of interference of this type can be eliminated by bonding or connecting all the metal components in a hull together electrically with a bonding wire (ordinary insulated wire is sufficient). This will also eliminate galvanic corrosion of all the metal parts so connected, except the one which is the most anodic metal on the galvanic scale. This one can corrode quite rapidly when immersed in an electrolyte (e.g. salt water again) whilst 'protecting' the others.

This principle of protection is widely used on full size craft operating continuously in salt water. Here a special *sacrificial anode* of high purity zinc is introduced into the bonded system on the hull bottom where it is continuously immersed in water. It is, of course, quite unnecessary on models, but *bonding* can be useful to eliminate strong galvanic currents being generated.

The Galvanic Scale

Having seen that the more widely separated metals are on the galvanic scale the more rapidly they can corrode when in contact with each other in the presence of salt spray or salt water, the following table of metals is a significant guide to material selection. If dissimilar metals have to be used for components used on, say, the mechanical side of a radio control system, choose those closest together on the galvanic scale (or similar metals if possible). This will minimise both galvanic currents and corrosion problems for boats operating in salt water. Such precautions are not necessary for boats operating in fresh water.

If you do have to use dissimilar metals in contact, then make sure that the most anodic (on the galvanic scale) has the larger *area.* This will minimise corrosive effects. Thus a stainless steel screw would be quite satisfactory holding a large aluminium fitting or plate; but a brass screw holding a stainless steel plate would tend to corrode rapidly.

The Galvanic Scale

Anodic end or most 'active' electro-chemically

↑

	Potential
Magnesium & magnesium alloys	1.6
Zinc	1.1
Galvanised iron	1.0
Aluminium & aluminium alloys	0.8–1.0
Cadmium plating (on steel)	0.8
Iron & mild steel	0.7–0.8
Cast iron (Grey)	0.7
Stainless steel (Active)	
18/8 and various types	0.46–0.57
Lead	0.55
Tin & Tinned steel	0.5
18/10/3 Stainless steel (Active)	0.35–0.45
Chromium plating	0.25–0.45
Brasses	0.3–0.4
Solder (Lead/tin)	0.28–0.36
Copper	0.30–0.36
Manganese bronze	0.28–0.32
Silicon bronze	0.26–0.29
Gunmetal	0.3
Stainless steel (Passive) various types	0.25–0.35
Tin bronze	0.24–0.31
Copper-nickel— 90:10	0.22–0.28
80:20	0.21–0.27
70:30	0.17–0.23
Nickel aluminium bronze	0.15–0.22
Silver solder	0.10–0.20
Stainless steel (Passive)	
18/8 and various types	0.05–0.10
Monel 400, monel K500	0.4–0.13
18/10/3 Stainless steel (Passive)	0.04–0.10
Silver	
Titanium	
Platinum & gold	

↓

Cathodic end or most noble or passive electro-chemically.

Note: when two dissimilar metals are in contact and wetted with any solution which is an active electrolyte (e.g. salt water) the more *anodic* metal will corrode.

OFFICIAL CLASSES FOR RADIO CONTROLLED BOATS

(a) POWERBOATS

For record and/or racing events there are four separate *categories* officially recognised for power boats. Each category is divided into separate *classes*. It is under these classes that National and International contests are run, and in which British and International records are established. Some model powerboat clubs may introduce their own classes for local events, but in the main encourage building models to official classes.

Class specifications are extensive and can only be surveyed briefly here. Detailed information can be obtained from the Secretary of the Model Power Boat Association; the (British) national authority. The name and address of the current secretary can always be obtained by contacting the editor of an appropriate model magazine (e.g. Model Boats, Box 35, Hemel Hempsted, Herts. Phone 0442 41221).

F1. Speed Classes

(F1)–V2.5—for boats powered by internal combustion engines up to 2.55cc displacement.
(F1)–V5—for boats with i/c engine 2.5–5cc displacement.
(F1)–V15—for boats with i/c engine 5–15cc displacement.
(F1)–1 kg—for boats powered by electric motors and having a total weight not exceeding 1 kilogram.
(F1)–E-500—for boats powered by electric motors limited to a maximum voltage of 42 volts. No limit on boat weight.

F2. Scale Models

The F2 class, covering scale models to be used for steering and docking contests is subdivided into different model sizes.

F3. Steering

F3V—for boats powered by internal combustion engines.
F3E—for boats powered by electric motors.

FSR Multi-Racing

This category covers boats which are raced simultaneously over a specified course. There are two main classes.

FSR-15—for boats powered by glow engines up to 15cc displacement

FSR-30—for boats powered by spark-ignition engine up to 30cc displacement.

There are also further sub-classes for boats powered by 3.5cc, 6.5cc, and 10cc engines; and electric motors.

(b) MODEL YACHTS

Here it is even more important for the modeller wishing to take part in yacht racing to select a *class* design which conforms to National rules and so *can* be raced. Quite a number of yacht designs, for example, do not fit into any recognised class and, unlike most powerboats, cannot be adapted to conform to any class specification. Note also that some kit models of *foreign* class designs again do not necessarily conform to British class requirements. A particular example is the American 36/600 class yacht which has no restriction on beam or depth of hull, whereas the equivalent British (36) class specification does set limits for beam and depth.

Official British classes for radio controlled yachts recognised by the Model Yachting Association are based on the free sailing classes prefixed with the letter R.

R36 Class

The smallest official class where maximum length is 36 in, maximum beam 9 in. and maximum depth 11 in. (The hull must fit inside a box with internal dimensions of 36 × 9 × 11 in.) Maximum weight in full racing trim must not exceed 12 lb. There are no restrictions on the size of sails.

RM or Marblehead Class

This is the most popular class. The specification calls for a maximum overall length of 50 in, and a maximum sail area of 800 sq. in. There are no restrictions on beam, depth or weight; but some minor regulations apply.

R6 (6 metre)

Normally scaled on the lines of a full size racing yacht, the R6 class give a hull length of about 60–66 in with a sail area of 1,100 to 1,200 sq. in. Displacement is of the order of 30–33 lb. It is not a class which finds popular support.

R10R (10 Rater)

A larger class of yacht which must conform to special rules, length is approximately 6 ft. with a narrow beam and a sail area of around 1,100 sq. in. Displacement is of the order of 25–30 lb.

RA ('A' Class)

Another large class built to a special formula. Length is normally between 6 and 7 feet with a sail area of around 1,650 sq. in. Displacement may range from 50 lb. up to 90 lb.

Although the first to be recognised by the National Yachting Association as a radio class, (when it was originally designated 'Q' class), its larger size and extremely heavy weight strictly limits its following.

Most model yacht clubs sail and race one particular class. If one particular class appeals to you, join a club which has adopted this class. If you join a local club, build and sail the class used by that club. In either case you will find sailing an R/C yacht far more enjoyable than trying to operate as a lone hand.

'SPOT' FREQUENCY COLOUR CODES (27 MHz working)

The frequency band allocated for use by radio control modellers in the U.K. (and known as the 27 MHz band) covers the transmitting frequency range 26.970 to 27.255 megahertz (MHz). A further frequency band within the 35 MHz spectrum has also recently been made available to modellers in the U.K., but this is primarily (or even exclusively) intended for model aircraft operators.

All modern radio transmitters are of superhet type, crystal controlled, enabling them to be operated on different 'spot' frequencies within this band. By working on different 'spot' frequencies several transmitters can be operated simultaneously.

For optimum separation of signals, six different 'spot' frequencies can be used, designated by a colour code. The idea behind this code is that the operator attaches a pennant to his transmitter aerial indicating the colour, and thus the 'spot' he is working on. Other operators can then work their equipment at the same time by choosing a different 'spot' (i.e. if necessary changing the transmitter and receiver crystals to give a different spot frequency for working).

Refinements in circuit design have made it possible to utilise more 'spot' frequencies mid-way between the 'standard' spots, giving a total of twelve spot frequencies in all in the 27MHz band. These are popularly known as split frequencies and are designated by a 'split' (i.e. two-colour) colour code.

Theoretically, at least, further 'splits' are possible with *FM* radio operating in the 27MHx band, giving an even greater number of 'spot' frequencies. As yet, however, FM operation is limited to the twelve 'spot' frequencies used for *AM* radio.

Spot	Spot Frequency* (Tx crystal frequency)	Colour Code
1	26.975	grey/brown
2	26.995	brown
3	27.025	brown/red
4	27.045	red
5	27.070	red/orange
6	27.095	orange
7	27.125	orange/yellow
8	27.145	yellow
9	27.175	yellow/green
10	27.195	green
11	27.225	green/blue
12	27.255	blue

*Note: Actual frequencies may vary slightly with different makes of set. This has no significance to the operator since his equipment will be working with a matched receiver crystal. However, operation on split frequencies can, at times, cause interference with other makes of equipment on the nearest standard spot frequency.

There is another frequency band available for model radio control in the U.K. This is the 459 MHz or UHF band (nominally 458.550 Hz to 459.450 MHz). This is capable of providing an even greater number of individual 'spot' frequencies within the band.

At present the availability of UHF sets for radio control is limited. Spot frequencies are referred to by Channel number (Channel 1, Channel 2, etc. . . . up to Channel 32). There is no corresponding colour coding, the actual operating frequency in use being quoted (or displayed by a marker) as the channel number.